"Concise, compelling, and complete . . . a brilliantly communicated resource on a critically important issue: the power communication. I recommend it to every woman who wants to hone her skills in this area."
**—Anne L. Bryant, executive director,
American Association of University Women**

◆

"Provides a play-by-play methodology for improving an individual's presentation skills . . . can dramatically improve perceptions about performance."
**—Diane B. Glossman, CFA vice president,
Salomon Brothers**

◆

"A valuable resource for anyone looking to get ahead and achieve success."
**—Paul J. Greeley, president of the American Chamber of
Commerce Executives**

◆

"An extremely useful compendium of communication strategies and techniques of interest to both men and women."
**—Barry L. Sherman, Ph.D., professor, journalism and
mass communications, University of Georgia**

◆

"Will help women to further develop their areas of natural ability: communication, organization, team building . . . [and] that needed amount of self-confidence to move into positions of leadership in any setting."
**—Carolyn Desjardins, Ph.D., executive director,
National Institute for Leadership Development**

MORE POWER TO YOU!

HOW WOMEN CAN COMMUNICATE
THEIR WAY TO SUCCESS

CONNIE BROWN GLASER AND
BARBARA STEINBERG SMALLEY

WARNER BOOKS

A Time Warner Company

WARNER BOOKS EDITION

Warner Books, Inc.
1271 Avenue of the Americas
New York, NY 10020

A Time Warner Company

Ⓦ Printed in the United States of America

First Trade Printing: March 1995

10 9 8 7 6 5 4 3 2 1

ISBN: 0-446-67070-7
LC: 94-62169

Cover design by Karen Katz
Cover photo by Joanne Savio

To Tom, Rusty, and Max for their love and support. And to my parents, Dolly and Bernie Brown, who encouraged me to become a power communicator.

Connie Brown Glaser

To Tim, Logan, and Benjamin and to my parents, Zelda and M.K., for their love, encouragement, and support and for always believing in me.

Barbara Steinberg Smalley

Acknowledgments

We are grateful to many people who made important contributions to this book. Bob Katz recognized early on the value of this project and provided us with guidance in its initial stages. George Greenfield, our agent, and Scott Sanders handled the negotiations, allowing us to concentrate on producing our best work. Joann Davis, our editor, believed in the book from the beginning. Her insights were intelligent and constructive, and we are indebted to her for her support and excellent ideas. We also appreciate Daphne Hall, Brenda Maggs Walsh, Quinton Phillips, David Rogers and staff at Kinko's for their quality service, enthusiasm, and great sense of humor ("You want it when?").

Special thanks to friends and colleagues who offered encouragement from inception to completion: Joan Arazie, Paula Balsley, Robin Chasman, Judy and Dan Hees, Krys Keller, Freddy Loef, Betty and Norton Melaver, Karen Robinson, Marcia Stamell, Gail and Kim Stearman, Andrew Vedlitz, Sally Willkens, and Susan Zalkind. Also, appreciation to Carol Deutsch for her simul-support. And to Sharon Loef, our "manager," whose devotion and enthusiasm have far exceeded her job description.

This book could not have been possible without the unwavering love and support of our families. They believed in us. They believed in the project. And they believed in our ability to get the job done. Our deepest gratitude to our husbands, Tom and Tim, and to our children, Rusty and Max, Logan and Benjamin, for their patience and reinforcement. We are grateful to our parents, Dolly and Bernie and Zelda and M. K., for their encouragement and enthusiasm. Thanks, too, to the Hawkins family for use of the Hawk's Nest and to Dale for her cheerleading and baby-sitting services.

We are indebted to the many women who answered our questionnaires and who have attended our seminars. Their overwhelming interest provided us with the inspiration to write this book. Special thanks to Opal Haley and June Cooke at The University of Georgia.

The decision to co-author this book emerged from a friendship that soon evolved into a dynamic partnership. From the start, power communications was a topic important to both of us. We were driven by the need to share our ideas with other working women. And by building upon each other's strengths, we found writing this book a labor of love.

Connie Brown Glaser and Barbara S. Smalley

Contents

Introduction

"Once power was considered a masculine attribute.
In fact, power has no sex."

Katherine Graham

• Sandy graduated three years ago from Yale. Her references include a letter from a superior court judge. Yet, Sandy has been stuck in a dead-end job as an administrative assistant for nearly two years.

"Six months ago, I registered with an employment agency, and several times they've called me with opportunities," she says. "But the scenario is always the same. They send over my résumé, and the client responds with great enthusiasm. In fact, more than once, I've gone into an interview situation as the top candidate. But I've yet to receive a single offer."

Recently, Sandy's employment agency counselor suggested that she sharpen her interviewing skills. "I went to a workshop where they video-taped me during a mock interview," she says, "and I was horrified at the results! I spoke too softly, displayed no confidence, and—worst of all—

I kept looking down and playing with my engagement ring!''

• Gail, a technical writer, was originally hired to work as an editor for a large engineering firm. Six months into the job, however, her supervisor became ill and had to take a medical leave of absence. When Gail was tapped to step in temporarily and take her boss's place, she was thrilled. "I felt honored to be asked," she says, "and was determined to do a good job. Of course, I knew it would entail a lot of extra work, but I felt like this was my chance to shine."

In addition to taking work home with her on weekends, Gail began putting in twelve-hour days at the office. "It was exhausting but exhilarating," she recalls, "and I was getting excellent feedback from the firm's owners."

Within six months, Gail's supervisor returned to work, and Gail resumed her position as editor. "It was tough going back to my old job, but at least I did so knowing that I'd made a good impression," she says. Indeed, all three of the firm's owners sent her notes of thanks for a job well done. "I not only treasured those letters," she says, "I decided to use them to get a raise or a bonus."

Rather than make an appointment to discuss her wishes, however, Gail stopped by the office of one of the owners one morning on the spur of the moment and blurted out, "I know you're really busy, and I have no idea what shape the firm's budget is in, but I know you all think I did a good job filling in for Nancy—because I have your letters to prove it—and I was hoping you would consider compensating me for that. What do you think?"

• Janet has worked as an insurance claims adjuster for eight years, "just waiting for my supervisor to retire," she says. "When he did last month, I applied for his position. I felt confident that nobody was more qualified for the position, and my interview went well—or so I thought. Imagine my surprise when the promotion went, instead, to a male co-worker who had been here less than two years!"

Janet spent weeks trying to determine why she'd been passed over for the promotion, then decided to confront her boss. "He assured me that I was a first-rate worker," she reports, "but he said I didn't get the job because I don't project the right image for a managerial position."

Landing a good job. Securing a raise. Being tapped for a promotion. No matter how good you look on paper, or how productive and dedicated you are, your communication skills will almost always be the deciding factor. In a survey of five hundred executives conducted by Communispond, Inc., communication skills ranked second only to job knowledge as factors crucial for business success. And when we say communication skills, we are referring to a host of factors, both verbal and nonverbal. Your speech patterns. Your mannerisms. The tone and quality of your voice. The gestures you use. The way you dress. The way you write. Your posture. Your eyes. Your facial expressions. Your listening skills. The questions you ask. Your sense of humor.

Collectively, these factors make up your professional image—how you're viewed by those in power when you apply for a job, ask for a raise, or try for a promotion. And if you're like most women, you are strong in some of these areas, but weaker in others. Which leads us to the primary thrust of this book: *To achieve positions of power, women must be able to communicate with power.*

How do we define power? We view it as the ability to get things accomplished—not by controlling and dominating others, but by influencing and motivating them. Power, in this sense, relies on cooperation instead of confrontation, and on establishing connections with others instead of controlling them. It is this kind of power that not only allows individuals to take charge of their own lives, but enables them to empower others. And for those who possess this kind of power, there are rich rewards: a strong sense of credibility, self-respect, and the support of others.

Why the focus on women? Because men are naturals at communicating with clout, thanks to social conditioning. And because the rules are often different for men. Here is a case in point. There's nothing wrong if a man is considered aggressive; in fact, it's complimentary. But if a woman is aggressive, it's unbecoming. Some will say, "She's a bitch," or "She's too masculine." Finally, despite the advances working women have made in the last two decades, there are still some lingering stereotypes we must contend with. Preconceived notions like: we're less intelligent than men; we're not confident; we don't know how to play the game; we try too hard; we're just tokens; we're not career oriented.

The good news is that women *are* capable of learning how to communicate with power and conviction. But to do so we must *unlearn* the submissive patterns we've been reared on. We must also be aware of the special barriers that exist due to age-old stereotypes and how, as a result of social conditioning, we (often unwittingly) reinforce these stereotypes and, consequently, give away power.

Master the language of power, and you can turn negatives into positives. Acquire the necessary skills to clear the obstacles that exist for today's working women, and you emerge a competent, assertive woman who commands respect. Combine your new skills with the many positive traits women have long been recognized for—creativity, tactfulness, a knack for building relationships, poise, good listening skills, to name a few—and you position yourself for great things!

Connie Brown Glaser and Barbara S. Smalley

CHAPTER I

In The Beginning

"Men are taught to apologize for their weaknesses, women for their strengths."

Lois Wyse

Sugar and spice and everything nice . . . it's what little girls were supposedly made of—or at least it represented the kind of behavior that was expected of us. For "little ladies," arguing, cursing, and showing anger were taboo. Instead, we were raised to be polite, cooperative, and docile. We were also encouraged to speak softly, always say please and thank-you, and smile a lot. Is it any wonder, then, that when we grew up, we found it difficult to express ourselves forcefully? Early social conditioning affects both men and women and explains many of the things we say and do as adults. The chart that follows describes contrasts in "typical" male and female behaviors.

Sex Role Conditioning: Why You Say and Do the Things You Do

"Typical" of Female Behavior	"Typical" of Male Behavior
Prefers playing in small groups or in pairs where intimacy is the key	Prefers playing in large groups that are structured hierarchically
Focus in childhood is on individual play (dolls, ballet, etc.)	Focus in childhood is on team play (baseball, football, etc.)
Waits to be chosen	Creates visibility for self
Plays to exercise or socialize	Plays to win
Self-reliant; believes, "If I want something done, I'll do it myself."	Relies on others; believes, "Delegate!"
Reluctant to complain; avoids confrontation	States grievances directly
Focuses more on day-to-day problems	Anticipates problems, generates alternatives
Thin-skinned, sensitive to criticism	Thick-skinned; expects criticism and views it as helpful
Excels at carrying out plans	Excels at developing plans
Passive	Initiates
Expects to do worse than in the past	Expects to do well, regardless of the past
Discounts strengths	Capitalizes on strengths
Emotional under pressure	Cool under pressure
Slow to resolve differences; often holds grudges	Resolves differences quickly; rarely holds grudges

"Typical" of Female Behavior	"Typical" of Male Behavior
Thinks in terms of "the way it ought to be"	Thinks in terms of "the way it is"
Attributes success to luck, fate—"I was in the right place at the right time."	Attributes success to self; believes, "I did it."
Focuses on costs of risks	Focuses on benefits of risks
Hopes and waits for promotion	Actively pursues promotion
Uncomfortable with pulling rank; prefers cooperating	Comfortable giving orders
Hopes to be successful	Expects to be successful
Believes, "I can't work with people I don't like, it's phoney."	Works with whoever is necessary; does not base relationships on personalities
Believes, "This is who I am, take it or leave it."	Determines, "What does the boss want?" Views fulfilling boss's expectations as game playing; has no qualms adopting a different style if it means getting ahead.

When does social conditioning begin? A number of studies suggest as early as birth. For example, social psychologist Jeffrey Rubin and his associates found that first-time fathers often choose different adjectives to describe their newborns, depending on whether the infants are boys or girls. Words and phrases fathers typically used to describe their day-old sons included "firm," "strong," "well-coordinated," and "alert." Adjectives fathers used to describe their newborn daughters ranged from "soft" and "weak" to "delicate" and "awkward."

In another study, researchers observed five mothers taking turns playing individually with "Adam," a six-month-old infant dressed in blue. Later, six different mothers were observed playing with "Beth," the same infant, then dressed in pink. Isolated in a room and given three toys (a plastic fish, a doll, and a train) for entertaining the infants, most mothers chose the train to entertain "Adam" and the doll to entertain "Beth." The mothers also interacted differently with the infants, depending on whether they thought they were playing with a girl or a boy. "Beth," for example, received more smiles and hugs than "Adam" did. Yet, in post-observation interviews, all eleven mothers said they believed infants should be treated in the same way.

As infants grow into toddlers, many parents continue to interact with their children in different ways. With sons, rough-and-tumble play is a favorite pastime; with daughters, the emphasis is less on playing and more on talking—with parents often using a singsong voice. When little boys are loud and boisterous, parents may excuse their behavior by rationalizing, "He's a boy!" But when girls act in the same way, they are more likely to be reprimanded with a "Little ladies don't talk that way!"

Sex-role expectations taught by parents are often reinforced in children's literature. Studies show that picture books and grade-school textbooks have traditionally featured more stories about males than females (a ratio of 95 to 1 in one study!). And in one analysis of fifty-eight picture books used by children's literature teachers at Eastern Michigan University, 84 percent of the books portraying women showed them wearing aprons. Pictures of women not wearing aprons included a nun, a queen, an Indian squaw, and a mother on an outing with her children.

Of course, teachers also play a significant role. In her study of preschool instructors, psychologist Lisa Serbin found that many had a tendency to foster dependency in girls. Instructors required girls—but not boys—to seek help when frustrated with a task.

Children learn gender-appropriate behavior from the mass media as well. Scores of studies have shown that men are more visible and enjoy higher status than women both on television and in films. Newspapers and magazines also tell us more about men than about women. On Saturday morning, even children's cartoons reinforce stereotypes. One study, for example, found that male cartoon characters are typically "adventuresome," "knowledgeable," "independent," and "aggressive," whereas female characters tend to be "submissive," "emotional," "fragile," and "timid."

In advertising, the trend is similar. Granted, the image of women both on television commercials and in print ads has improved dramatically in the last decade. Historically, however, men have been depicted as competent, aggressive, and powerful, while women have been portrayed either as sex objects or as housewives obsessed with cleanliness.

As a result of all this early social conditioning—from parents, schools, and the mass media—boys and girls emerge with very different self-concepts. And these differences later surface not only in the ways they play, but in the ways they communicate.

Boys, for example, prefer to play outside in large groups that are structured hierarchically (baseball, soccer, tag). Their groups typically have a leader, and their games almost always have winners and losers. Boys also like to boast about their skills and argue about who's best at what.

Girls, on the other hand, prefer playing in small groups or in pairs, where intimacy is the key. In their most popular games (house, jump rope, hopscotch), everyone gets a turn, and there are no winners or losers. Rarely do they boast about who's better, challenge each other, or vie for status. They are far more concerned with being liked. In fact, one of their favorite activities involves just sitting together and talking.

When boys play and one gets hurt, the others will usually drag him off the field and continue to play. For them, the game is more important than the individual players. Girls, however, will usually stop a game until the injured player recovers. For them, the individual players take priority over the game.

When someone disputes the rules in a boys' game, the others are likely to say something like, "Either you play by our rules, or get out of the game." Yet, when someone suggests a better idea about the rules in a girls' game, there is a tendency for everyone to discuss the idea, change some of the rules, and try a new version of the game.

Boys at play issue commands without giving reasons for them. "I'm captain today . . . Ted is on my team; you can have Doug." In contrast, girls make proposals by saying, "Let's . . ." followed by reasons for their suggestions. It's their way of avoiding confrontation.

Boys rarely hesitate to complain to others face-to-face. They are also more apt to state their grievances directly. Girls, however, typically complain in the *absence* of the accused— again, to avoid confrontation. They are also more likely to work out complex alliances with each other, and often against one another.

When boys fight during games, they are able to resolve their differences quickly and effectively. In fact, one study found that boys seem to enjoy debating as much as they do the game itself. In contrast, arguments among girls not only tend to end their games, they often last for weeks and can lead to realignments within social groups.

So what happens when boys and girls grow up and enter

the work force? For starters, men slide comfortably into hier-archical structures—after all, they were reared on them. Women, on the other hand, prefer cooperating with people rather than controlling them or being controlled *by* them. Men have no qualms about issuing orders or voicing complaints. Women, however, are uncomfortable with pulling rank and prefer to get their way by having everyone agree. Men handle disagreements with aplomb, oftentimes relishing the opportunity to express themselves. Women, on the other hand, typically go out of their way to avoid confrontation.

Finally, men *expect* to be successful, and when they are, take full credit. In contrast, women *hope* to be successful, and when they are, often attribute it to luck or to the collaboration of others.

Whose style is better? Traditionally, the male model of authority was considered superior. Macho equaled power. However, power communicators recognize that there are strengths and weaknesses associated with both styles. They also know that the real key to success lies not only in understanding the difference between the two, but in focusing on a style that encompasses the best of *both* worlds.

CHAPTER 2

Speech Patterns That Give You Away

"Act apologetic and you will lose.
Act certain and you will win."
Robert Pante

Since early social conditioning teaches women to speak like "little ladies," this can later translate into speech patterns that are less incisive and more submissive than men's. As a result, we often jeopardize our chances at being taken seriously or being viewed as professionals.

Listen in for a minute to this conversation:

Boss: I asked you to have that report on my desk by the time I got back in town. Where is it?

Secretary: I'm *so* sorry, sir. You are probably not going to be very happy about this, but, well, while you were gone, two secretaries called in sick—one had a family emergency when her daughter fell off the jungle gym at school, and the other came down with the flu, or whatever it is that is going around. And,

you know the office has just been *so* busy
lately. Somebody had to fill in, so I did what
was necessary to hold down the fort. I knew
you would want it that way. Aren't I right?

This conversation illustrates the most common speech patterns that can undermine our credibility:

Excessive Apologies

The secretary in the above example opens her response with an apology—a tactic women use more frequently than men and often carry to the extreme. Naturally, if you've wronged someone, an apology is appropriate, but *there's no need to apologize for your thoughts, feelings, or a situation over which you have no control.* When you do, it not only takes the punch out of your statements, it detracts from your credibility.

Here's another example. Gail, an office manager in her mid-thirties, says, "It's amazing the number of times I catch myself saying I'm sorry for something that isn't my fault. Just yesterday, my boss needed a report by a certain time, and I was unable to deliver it because the computer was down. But instead of explaining the problem to him, I went into his office and started apologizing profusely, like *I* was the one to blame!"

The computer snafu was not Gail's fault; therefore, she didn't need to apologize. The same holds true for the secretary in our example. But by apologizing, both women made it appear as if the failure to complete their bosses' reports on time was their fault. A better approach? State the problem up-front and leave out the apology altogether. The secretary, for example, might say, "Because we were short staffed and

the office was busy, I had to rearrange my priorities." And
Gail might say, "Since the computer was down, the information I needed to complete your report was unavailable." Rephrasing responses in this way transfers the blame from you
to the *real* cause of a problem.

Hedging or Use of Qualifiers

After apologizing, the secretary in our example continues,
"You are probably not going to be very happy about this,
but, well . . ." Words like *well, y'know, kinda*, and *sorta*
and phrases such as *I think, I guess, I suppose, you may not
agree with me, but . . .* or *I'm not 100 percent sure, but . . .*
make us sound weak, uncertain, and uncommitted to what
we are saying. Here is a case in point. Remove the qualifiers
(in italics) and compare the force in these statements: "*Perhaps* I need more training to accomplish my goals"; "I *wonder if* you should chair that meeting instead of me"; *It seems
to me that* I deserve a raise."

Yet, qualifiers are legitimate in certain situations—for example, when you *are* uncertain about what you are saying.
When you use them, however, you needn't come across
sounding timid and passive. Instead, say what you have to
say with a firm voice, and avoid dropping your head or avert-
ing your eyes. Otherwise, the person you're speaking to may
mistake your uncertainty for helplessness.

Excessive Chitchat

The secretary goes on to explain, ". . . while you were
gone, two secretaries called in sick—one had a family emergency when her daughter fell off the jungle gym at school,

and the other came down with the flu, or whatever it is that is going around." A number of studies have found that women disclose more personal information in their speech than men do. While sharing personal details has its positive aspects—makes you appear friendly and encourages others to open up—too much self-disclosure in the workplace can turn people off. If you have an anecdote to share that relates to the topic you are discussing with someone, share it, but keep it brief. Otherwise, save personal stories for friends and family members.

For example, Jessica, a social worker with ten years of experience, recently decided to ask her supervisor for a raise. "We'd been short staffed for nearly a year, and I'd been working a lot of overtime," she says. "I knew the budget was tight, but I felt I deserved a raise." Yet, when her supervisor asked Jessica to document the reasons she felt she should receive a pay increase, Jessica wrote a lengthy sob story explaining how her husband had recently been forced to take a cut in pay, how she had exceeded the limit on all her credit cards, and how much her daughter's upcoming wedding was going to cost.

Not surprisingly, Jessica was denied a raise—and with good reason. She used the wrong approach in her attempts to justify a pay increase. Salaries are linked to job performance, not personal family needs. Had Jessica highlighted her professional accomplishments instead of expounding on her family problems, she might have merited a raise.

Empty Adjectives and Adverbs

Some adverbs tend to have a fluffing effect on our messages, particularly when they are used to emphasize our feelings, as in the secretary's statement, "And you know, the

office has *just* been so busy lately.'' Other empty adverbs to
watch out for include *such, awfully,* and *terribly.* ''It was
such a difficult assignment!'' ''I had an *awfully* good time at
the convention. I feel *terribly* bad that I can't attend the
meeting.''

Certain adjectives—like *sweet, precious,* and *tiny* (or
worse, *teeny-tiny*) also lack clout and substance because they
are frilly words typically associated with women. To say that
someone is *so sweet* or *just precious* or to suggest that a co-
worker correct a *teeny-tiny* mistake he made on a report can
make you sound girlish and unprofessional. More powerful—
and genderless—descriptive words include: *absolutely, re-
markably,* and *incredibly* (adverbs) and *excellent, outstanding,* and *terrific* (adjectives).

Tag Questions

A tag takes a firm and decisive statement and turns it
into an unnecessary question. The secretary in our example
concludes with one. ''. . . so I did what was necessary to
hold down the fort. I knew you would want it that way. Aren't
I right?''

As women, we typically want to avoid confrontation. Consequently, we use tags in an effort to please everyone or to
get others to buy into our agenda. In fact, most of us use tags
without thinking, but overuse of them can make us appear
wishy-washy and incapable of making decisions.

Theresa's story is another good example. A junior advertising executive whose goal is to win the account of an up-and-
coming pharmaceutical company, Theresa and her staff spend
months putting together an elaborate multimedia campaign.
When she shares the group's efforts with the potential client,
her presentation is flawless. And as she winds up her speech,

the majority of her audience appears mesmerized by her ideas. In closing, however, she tilts her head slightly to one side and adds, "This could work, I think—don't you agree?"

How can you avoid using tag questions? Concentrate on lowering your voice at the end of each sentence. And have enough confidence in yourself not to ask the question.

The problem is that sometimes tag questions are legitimate—when seeking confirmation because you've missed seeing or hearing all that someone has said ("Dr. Smith is coming to the meeting, isn't she?"); when trying to break the ice ("Sure is hot, isn't it?"); or when you are requesting confirmation for something you hope will happen ("It's all right if I use the company car, isn't it?"). *But avoid tag questions when you're talking about your opinions.* Otherwise, you give the impression that you're not sure of yourself.

Disclaimers

Introductory expressions that excuse, explain, or request understanding ("I'm probably wrong, but . . ."; "You may not like this, but . . ."; "I suppose we could . . ."; "Maybe this is okay . . .") not only strip you of power, they invite listeners to disagree. Disclaimers also dramatically decrease a speaker's level of influence—particularly when that speaker is a woman. In fact, research indicates that when women use tag questions and disclaimers, subjects judge them as less intelligent and knowledgeable than men who also use them.

Lengthy Requests

Powerful people know what they want to say and say it concisely and precisely. Thus, when speaking the language of power, keep this rule of thumb in mind: the shorter a request, the more force it conveys. "I want tomorrow off" is a power request; "I really hate to bother you, because I know you're busy, but do you think it would be okay if I took tomorrow off?" is not.

Superpolite Speech

Because women are reared on polite language, we emerge experts at using euphemisms and at saying "please" and "thank-you" excessively. We also tend to use fewer contractions and to be overly cautious about using slang words. Where does it get us? Nowhere. Instead of building respect and status, superpolite speech can give us an uptight image. Furthermore, when we focus too much on sounding grammatically correct, the point we're trying to make often gets lost.

Here's a good before and after example. "I would certainly appreciate it if you could please tell John, whom I spoke with yesterday, that due to unforeseen circumstances, I cannot attend the meeting." A better way: "Please tell John I can't attend the meeting."

Self-effacing Remarks

Women have a tendency to put themselves down—particularly when they are put on the spot. When Susan, a clerk in a large insurance company, recently had her yearly performance review, her boss's first question was, "How do you think you've done this year?" The question caught Susan off guard, and instead of citing her many accomplishments, she replied, "I don't know. I suppose I could have done better. I've tried to do my best, but circumstances have been difficult at times.'' Later, Susan learned that her boss had considered giving her a promotion following her review, but after her self-defeating remarks, he couldn't justify it.

In her book, *You Just Don't Understand: Women and Men in Conversation*, Deborah Tannen, Ph.D., says that many women are reluctant to boast about their achievements to others because they fear people won't like them if they do. These feelings stem from a combination of social conditioning and peer pressure in childhood that it's not ladylike to be boastful. Yet, when women do not blow their own horns, they risk being underestimated by their superiors.

Fillers

We're all guilty of using fillers—particularly when caught in situations where we can't think of anything to say. But studies show that women use them in much higher proportions than men do. Not surprisingly, we tend to use fewer fillers in woman-to-woman conversations than we do when we address men—which has led researchers to theorize that women use fillers to offset or play down their intelligence or to allay their fear of coming on too strong. Fillers, however, signal uncertainty and lack of preparation. They also open the door to interruption.

Here's a quick hit list of fillers to avoid: *um, ah, like, well, uh, er, y'know, kinda,* and *sorta.*

Asking Too Many Questions

Studies have shown that women ask about three times as many questions as men. Not surprisingly, we do so more often in one-on-one situations with men—and for good reasons. In an effort to strike up a comfortable conversation, we ask questions until we've hit upon a subject men seem interested in. We also use questions to indicate our interest in a subject they've brought up. Asking questions is fine. It shows we're interested in details and want a thorough understanding of a situation. It also enables us to make better decisions. But, again, if you're so busy asking questions, you're not likely to get your own opinion out.

Women are also more likely to open a conversation with a question—a speech pattern that signals uncertainty and a desire for attention. Here are some examples. "Guess what happened today?" versus, "I got a promotion today." "Does everyone know why I called this meeting?" versus, "I called this meeting to discuss our new benefits package." And, "Is everyone aware that our sales are off this month?" versus, "We're all aware that sales are off this month."

Powerless Voice

Think "voice of authority," and more than likely a male image comes to mind. John F. Kennedy. Walter Cronkite. Jesse Jackson. Peter Jennings. Because men's voices are stronger and deeper than women's, they are more often associated with power. But that doesn't mean that women can't sound equally authoritative.

Granted, our voices are partially influenced by physiology. As Sandy Linver explains in *Speakeasy: How to Talk Your Way to the Top*, "Men's vocal cords are longer and thicker than women's, so men's natural pitch is lower. But within this natural range, the pitch many people use is not their optimum pitch, but is often the pitch determined by habit, imitation, or even by tension of the jaw." And any voice coach will tell you that you can learn to sound firmer, more relaxed, more assertive, and more confident. In fact, your voice is a key instrument in developing an authoritative communication style, so invest some time in evaluating yours by focusing on these elements:

Tone and Volume—A whispery voice lacks power, invites interruption, and implies lack of confidence. The same goes for a mumbling voice. A mousy squeak can signal helplessness and sound like a carry-over from your childhood days. A monotone not only puts people to sleep, but makes you sound totally disinterested in what you are saying. Since each of us has a range from high to low, practice until you find a pitch that is relatively low (but still comfortable) and sounds forceful.

Rate—Generally, the faster you speak, the higher your pitch will be. Moreover, speaking too fast can make you sound like you're babbling. You may also be perceived as nervous or overanxious. Speak too slowly, however, and you'll not only bore those who must listen to you, you'll imply that you are weak and uncertain. Go, instead, for an even, conversational tone.

Quality—Some of us (usually unconsciously) raise the pitch of our voice when we are nervous or when we are trying to gain a concession from someone in authority. That's a problem that can be corrected with practice. If, however, the normal voice you use is extremely high-pitched, and you have difficulty moderating it yourself, you should consider consulting a professional voice coach.

What steps can you take on your own to sound more authoritative? Voice coaches recommend focusing on breathing from the diaphragm with full, deep breaths, starting from the stomach and working up. Another good technique is to record your natural voice on tape and play it back, then record it again using a deeper pitch. "Pretend you're an important, powerful leader," offers Norma Carr-Ruffino, Ph.D., in her book *The Promotable Woman.* "As you listen to playbacks, be alert for voice tones that are apologetic, tentative, meek, or imploring." If all this feels too forced, try taping your telephone conversations instead, and see if you can pick up some voice patterns you want to change.

In his book, *You Are the Message: Getting What You Want By Being Who You Are*, Roger Ailes suggests another voice-improvement exercise he calls "tape and ape." Buy—or check out from the library—a cassette tape of a famous actor or actress giving a speech or reading a literary classic. After listening to it, record yourself reading those same selections and compare your vocal quality. "Your goal isn't to become a performer," Ailes says, "but when you hear good speech and attempt to emulate it, you *will* improve your voice."

Train yourself to use speech patterns that are conversational yet crisp, and you gain credibility. Match these with equally credible mannerisms, and you're well on your way to becoming a power communicator!

CHAPTER 3

Mannerisms To Make You A Heavyweight

"Facial expression is human experience rendered immediately visible."

Edmund Carpenter

One of the most revealing differences between powerful people and those with little or no power lies in nonverbal communication. Women are generally more animated and use more expressive gestures than men do. These are positive attributes because they enhance our communication effectiveness. However, they can often be our downfall—because our nonverbal messages speak louder than our words.

In a landmark study of communications, sociolinguist Albert Mehrabian discovered that:

- 7 percent of any message comes from the words we use,
- 38 percent comes from the voice we use, and
- 55 percent comes from our body language.

Mehrabian's formula had a startling impact on communications theory. A whopping 55 percent of our messages comes from something that is *unconscious* and has nothing to do with the words we use! In fact, when our facial expression or voice tone conflicts with our words, the listener will normally accept and act on the nonverbal message.

Take Ellen, who was recently appointed the first female board member of a large bank. "Initially, I was thrilled to be named to the board," she says. "But after the first few meetings, I began feeling discouraged because nobody ever asked my opinion on a subject." When Ellen expressed her concerns to a fellow board member, who was also her mentor, she discovered that her body language was the cause of her problem. "It seems that since I was constantly nodding or shaking my head, everyone assumed they *knew* what I thought," she reports.

When our body language makes us transparent, as in Ellen's case, we also surrender our power to negotiate effectively. For example, when Sandy, a telemarketing specialist, applied for a promotion, her interview went so well that she was offered the job on the spot. "I'd had my eye on that job for over a year, so naturally I was ecstatic," she recalls. "But I blew it by reacting to my boss's offer with too much enthusiasm. Once he sensed how excited I was, he knew I wasn't going to turn him down. Consequently, he offered me a lower salary than I'd hoped for. And while I managed to get him to raise the figure a little bit, I'm convinced I could have gotten more, had I contained my enthusiasm."

How can you match your nonverbal behavior to the powerful speech patterns you've mastered so far? Begin by keeping in mind these six mannerisms that can make you a lightweight:

Smiling too much and at inappropriate times

Studies reveal that women smile more than men do. Why? Since childhood, we have been taught not only to mask our negative feelings, but to "let a smile be our umbrella." And most women have learned this lesson well.

On the plus side, a smile can be an asset. It projects warmth, conveys confidence, and is a valuable tool for establishing rapport. However, smiling at inappropriate times—especially when it conflicts with your tone of voice or the words being spoken—can work against you by sending a mixed message. In fact, after researching women's smiling behavior for over a decade, Audrey Nelson-Schneider, Ph.D., a communications consultant in Boulder, Colorado, concludes that inappropriate smiling is the most common example of the way women's nonverbal behavior discounts their verbal messages. "When we are angry or we are trying to sell something, we want to be taken seriously," she says. "But then we smile." Inappropriate smiling can also make us appear weak and unassertive or can be misinterpreted as a sign of flirtatiousness.

Some women also have a habit of laughing at inappropriate times—when they are nervous, when they are introduced to someone and aren't sure what to say, or when they end their statements. But, like smiling, giggling can make you appear silly and girlish.

How can you avoid becoming a victim of what Nelson-Schneider calls the "Howdy-Doody Syndrome"? Monitor yourself for nervous grinning and giggling, and learn to keep a poker face in business situations—such as serious meetings and negotiations—where a smile may do you more harm than good.

Tilting or nodding the head

Watch for other small gestures that make you appear submissive—such as tilting your head to one side. Many of us do this without even realizing it; yet, it reinforces the cute little girl look—particularly when we're talking to men. And when accompanied by a tag question, the head tilt says you're indecisive. Head bobbing, usually done when listening, is another distracting habit. It can be particularly dangerous, since it indicates that you agree with what someone is saying—even when you may not!

Submissive body posture

Good posture conveys a sense of personal power, and research reported in *Live for Success* by John T. Molloy indicates that the most effective power stance for men and women is almost military: spine and head erect and straight, feet slightly spread, arms at sides with fingers slightly cupped. Thus, avoid slouching and hugging your chest with your arms. Also avoid standing with one or both hands on your hips. According to Molloy, this is a power stance for men but a nonpower stance for women.

When you are talking to a man who is taller than you, resist the urge to bend your head back or tilt it to one side. Instead, casually take a few steps backward until your gaze is level with his.

When you are sitting, refrain from clasping your hands tightly together, leaning forward, and looking down, because it can make you look nervous or submissive. Instead, place your elbows loosely on the arms of your chair, and occasionally lean to one side in a relaxed manner.

Distracting hand gestures

When you are trying to make a point and you twirl your hair, fiddle with an earring or bracelet, tap your pencil, cover your face, or pick at your cuticles, you send out the message that you are tense or uncertain. Instead, focus on using gestures to express confidence. Point. Punch the air with your fist. Steeple your hands, or rub them together briefly. These are power gestures. Also keep in mind that to be effective, gestures must match and confirm your words, not distract or contradict them, and that excessive or random gestures can diminish the strength of your delivery.

Avoiding eye contact

Good eye contact is perhaps the most important gesture a woman can master if she wants to be taken seriously. One study, for example, found that job applicants who engage in more eye contact are seen as more alert, dependable, confident, and responsible. In another study, only applicants who used an above-average amount of eye contact (accompanied by a high energy level, speech fluency, and voice modulation) were judged worth inviting back for a second interview. Besides, when you avoid establishing eye contact with someone, you not only signal submissiveness, you also invite interruption.

The rules for effective eye contact are simple. Never look down. Instead, maintain frequent eye contact whether you are talking or listening, but don't stare. Too much eye contact can signal anger, challenge, or sexual attraction. So, keep your gaze on the speaker steady and firm, but get (and give) some relief by looking away every few seconds.

Allowing the Invasion of Personal Space

Personal space—or the distance that is usually maintained between two people when they are sitting, standing, or talking—is highly significant in the business world. Studies show that powerful people take up more space and have fewer reservations about invading the space of others. In contrast, less powerful people tend to back off and yield space to others who are more powerful.

A word of caution here. We strongly advise *against* invading anyone else's personal space. While such behavior might make a man appear more powerful, it can make a woman appear overly aggressive. The best rule of thumb to keep in mind is to stay in the comfort zone by always maintaining an arm's length between you and the other person. And if someone tries to invade *your* personal space? You can hold your ground by not moving out of the way. However, if the proximity makes you uncomfortable, taking a few baby steps backward may increase your comfort level and help you maintain control. Or, suggest that the two of you sit down to continue your conversation. That way you can choose a seating arrangement that will put you in a position of power or equality.

A good way to pinpoint any mannerisms you have that need improvement is to stand in front of a mirror and observe what your hands, eyes, face, and posture are saying about you. Looking at photographs and watching videotapes of yourself are other viable alternatives for analyzing your body language. Regardless of the method you use, your goal should be to match your mannerisms to your verbal messages.

As you work on sharpening your skills, bear in mind that if your body language spells confidence and high status, others are more likely to view you that way. In one study, for example, psychologists asked subjects to pick out lower-status people. In most instances, the subjects based their judgments on nonverbal cues—like frequent nodding and smiling and holding the arms close to the body. Not surprisingly, more women than men exhibited these kinds of behaviors. Yet, when the same women deliberately exhibited more "high-status" behavior—smiling only occasionally, holding their heads comparatively still, and standing in a more relaxed posture, both men and women judged that they held high-status jobs—whether or not they actually did!

CHAPTER 4

Male Talk

"Slang is a language that rolls up its sleeves, spits on its hands, and goes to work."

Carl Sandburg

Communicating with clout does not mean trying to act like a man, although some women assume that it does. Yet, when women try to act macho, they are often alienated and ridiculed by subordinates, colleagues, and superiors of *both* sexes.

For example, when Margaret was promoted from an office manager to an administrator at the hospital where she'd worked since graduating from college, her management style changed.

As an office manager, she'd allowed her staff to work flexible hours whenever they or their family members had doctors' appointments or other commitments. She'd been accessible at all times, had kept her office door open to people with problems, and had placed a suggestion box in the employee break room. When employees were out sick or on vacation, she'd pitched in and helped the staff, and had never hesitated to ask questions about procedures she hadn't performed in a while. She had arranged quarterly luncheons to thank her staff for a job well done. And whenever her boss had mistreated a member of her staff, she had never hesitated to stick up for her employees.

With Margaret's new title, however, came self-imposed new rules. Although she hired an office manager to take her place, Margaret made it clear that she was still in charge of the department. Suddenly, medical appointments had to be scheduled before or after work. She began closing her office door, and requiring her office manager and other staff members to schedule appointments to discuss any problems. She abolished quarterly luncheons and discouraged the office manager from helping out the staff, regardless of how many were out sick or on vacation.

"That promotion meant the world to me," Margaret says, "and it was one I'd been working nearly ten years for. There was absolutely no way I was going to blow it. So I decided to emulate my boss, who manages with an iron fist. And while I'd be the first to admit that he's tough and difficult to work for, he's also one of the main decision makers in the hospital."

Three months following her promotion, Margaret's boss placed her on probation. "He claimed everyone was complaining that I'd gone from a confident and caring worker to a cold and critical workhorse," she says.

Margaret had been promoted because she was a competent manager. And she was competent because she was fair and caring with her staff. Once promoted, however, Margaret felt the need to change her management style. Noting how successful her boss was, she decided to use him as a role model—despite the fact that she detested his management style. But the switch-over from kind and cooperative to aloof and authoritarian didn't work. Margaret mistakenly equated success and power with macho behavior and, as a result, alienated both her staff and her superiors.

The style and language of power *have* been traditionally authoritarian. Fortunately, however, effective management style is changing, as we discuss later in Management Style. Nonetheless, powerful language continues to be firmly rooted in the male tradition.

As Betty Lehan Harragan points out in her book, *Games Mother Never Taught You*, the majority of business lingo is derived primarily from the male experience, with most of it coming from the military and sports (*bite the bullet, pulling rank, under the gun, carry the ball, ballpark figure, out in left field, team player*). She also believes that working women must learn to understand and translate this jargon correctly, or they will miss the deeper meaning and true significance of what's being said.

For example, soon after Laura was promoted to division manager for the computer consulting firm she worked for, she began attending regularly scheduled division manager meetings. "Being new at the job and the only woman at these meetings, I was nervous at first," she recalls. "But after a couple of months, I felt comfortable in my new role. Then something very embarrassing happened.

"One of our new clients was having trouble with the computer system we'd installed and was threatening to sue us. At one of our division meetings, we were discussing strategies for handling the problem—as well as details for a client luncheon we were hosting in our offices the next day—when our president suggested, 'We need to call Frank in to play cleanup.' Everyone else nodded in agreement. But I was confused and said, 'But our janitor's name is Rudy.' Everyone then turned to me and burst out laughing.

"As it turns out, the term 'cleanup' comes from baseball

and refers to the 'cleanup' hitter. This player is typically the team's power hitter and bats fourth in the team's batting lineup. Ideally, when he gets up to bat, the bases are loaded, and he hits a grand slam. In other words, he 'cleans up' the bases. In the business world, the 'cleanup' hitter is the firm's best player, or the person who is most knowledgeable in a specific area. And in my firm's situation, Frank, one of our vice-presidents, is apparently the one to call to fix complicated computer glitches.''

You're probably familiar with most of the lingo men use, but like Laura, you might be thrown a curve as to its usage in the business world.

Here are some examples to decipher. Compare your responses to the translations which follow the examples.

1. Maybe we misjudged their strength, but then it's easy to be a *Monday morning quarterback*.
2. Let's get someone besides Jones to pitch that idea. The last thing we need *at the helm* is a *loose cannon*.
3. We've hit a snag in our negotiations with Martin & Sawyer, Inc. Should we try to run an *end around* to advance our position?
4. Let's go to the *bullpen* to get some help on this.
5. I vote we give Clark a stab at the Carter account. Landing it should be a *layup*.
6. She's a definite possibility for *officer candidate school*.
7. Why did Jonathan get the company's box tickets to the Knicks game tomorrow night? I guess *RHIP*.
8. As for the bids we've currently received, the *leader in the clubhouse* is Smith & Wexler, Inc. with a bid of $6,900.
9. Craftsman, Inc. *spiked* my proposal this afternoon.
10. We're scheduled to pitch this proposal a week from

tomorrow. I'm expecting each of you to work separately, then let's plan to meet at the end of the week for a *SITREP*.

Translations

1. *Monday morning quarterback* is a football term referring to a player or spectator who's known for expounding on how something "should have been done" or "how I would have done it"—after the fact. In business situations, the Monday morning quarterback is the one who points out the obvious—after the fact—when a business venture has failed or not met expectations.

2. From the military, a *loose cannon* is someone who is unpredictable. Just as you never know where a loose cannon is going to fire, you never know what that person is going to say. *At the helm*, also derived from the military, refers to the person in charge.

3. *End around* is a football term that means to go in a different direction or to provide a distraction.

4. A baseball term, the *bullpen* is where relief pitchers warm up. In business, this means calling in someone fresh to finish the job.

5. *Layup* comes from basketball and refers to an easy shot, a sure shot. In business, it means something simple, a sure thing.

6. From the military, someone who is a possibility for *officer candidate school* is someone worthy of more training or someone who should be considered for a promotion.

7. Also from the military, *RHIP* stands for "Rank Has Its Privilege."

8. A golf term, the *leader in the clubhouse*, in this con-
   text, is the company with the highest bid thus far.
   This company is not necessarily the ultimate winner,
   however, as other higher bids may come in.
9. *Spiked* is a volleyball term. In business, it means to
   be rejected or shot down.
10. *SITREP* is a military acronym that stands for situation
    report.

Psychologist Harry Levinson adds that women can gain
insight into how men in authority communicate and manage
by reading the sports pages. "There's a bluntness to much of
sports reporting, a candor you don't get elsewhere," he says.
"Stories about how successful coaches motivate, evaluate,
and discipline players offer insight into management style and
philosophy, and you gain perspective about negotiating with
employees and handling disputes."

Another way to increase your business savvy is to learn to
play the games men play, but only if you feel comfortable
and confident in doing so. Looking for access to key players
in the political arena, Congresswoman Barbara B. Kennelly,
from Connecticut, decided to renew her interest in golf when
she went to Washington. On the putting greens she made
friends with Speaker of the House, Thomas "Tip" O'Neill.
Soon she was elected to the prestigious House Ways and
Means Committee. Only the third woman ever elected to sit
on that committee, Kennelly reportedly won out over the
objections of powerful chairperson Dan Rostenkowski. And
in 1991, Kennelly was selected as one of three chief deputy
majority whips in the U.S. House of Representatives, making
her the highest ranking woman in Congress.

Men also love poker—and with good reason. It trains players to think strategically. In fact, women who have mastered
this game claim that learning to play will clue you into a

whole other realm of business slang (*calling someone's bluff, cutting your losses, laying your cards on the table, upping the ante*). It will also enhance your willingness to take risks both at and away from the workplace.

Should you use male jargon yourself? By all means—*if* you know what you're talking about. If not, you'll sound phony. And whether you use male talk or not, it's critical to be familiar with it so you can understand what's going on. Otherwise, you may not make it to the majors.

CHAPTER 5

Podium Power

"When a man gets up to speak, people listen then look. When a woman gets up, people look; then, if they like what they see, they listen."

Pauline Frederick

Here's the scenario. The room is overflowing with smiling faces and anxious ears. Behind the podium someone is introducing you as the next speaker. Your lifetime achievements are proclaimed in a few moments' time, and the audience appears impressed and expectant. Your hands are moist, your throat parched, your knees shaky, and your heart pounding. Caterpillars are metamorphosing inside your stomach. Applause. You're on. You manage a weak smile, embrace the podium, and suddenly your mind goes totally blank.

If this scenario sounds uncomfortably familiar, you're in excellent company. Many of us view speech making as a terrifying experience and one to be avoided at all costs. Indeed, in David Wallachinsky, Irving Wallace and Amy Wallace's *Book of Lists* appears a survey of what some three thousand people say they most fear. Topping that list is "speaking before a group." To put that response in perspective, "death" trailed as response number six!

Nevertheless, public speaking is one of the best ways for women to create visibility and to gain credibility. In fact, the ability to speak well before a group not only gives you a competitive edge, it is critical for moving up and getting ahead. In one survey of four hundred businessmen and businesswomen, respondents were asked to list the top three traits they preferred in employees. Sixty-eight percent noted that they look for good speaking abilities.

What causes otherwise competent, rational, and intelligent women to stress-out when expected to give a speech or presentation? Chalk it up to social conditioning. As Deborah Tannen points out in *You Just Don't Understand: Women and Men in Conversation*, women are more comfortable talking when they are among friends and equals. Men, on the other hand, are generally more comfortable addressing groups of people, as it fulfills their need to establish and maintain status.

If, however, the mere thought of giving a speech or presentation sends chills down your spine, these tips should help you exorcise your fears as well as help you establish podium power:

• Think of speakers you've heard who have left you spellbound. What qualities did they possess? Warmth? Enthusiasm? Animation? An air of authority and conviction? Now think of those who have made you squirm in your seat with boredom and the qualities that made listening to them such a chore. Did they seem cold? Aloof? Nervous? Unenthusiastic? Powerful speakers connect with their audience by emitting a positive attitude both about themselves and the speech they are delivering. In short, they look as if they are enjoying themselves, and this is a skill you can master through preparation and practice.

• Preparation means doing your homework.

• Be familiar with your speaking environment. That way you can practice at home while visualizing the actual setting, which should help calm your nerves. You can also request a change in the layout if you are not satisfied.

• Get to know your audience as well. Find out as much as you can ahead of time about their ages, occupations, titles, and political beliefs. Also, arrive early to mingle among those you'll be addressing and introduce yourself to as many new faces as possible. That way you won't be addressing a room full of strangers.

• Find out what time you're speaking. If you're on after lunch, for example, do all you can to add pep and pizazz to your presentation, as an audience's attention span tends to plummet following a meal.

• If you're one of several speakers on a program, find out who else is speaking and what their topics are. If others' topics sound similar to yours, contact them in advance so you can avoid repetition.

• When asked to serve on a panel, ask the moderator for a list of names and telephone numbers of the other panelists. Contact each of them ahead of time to determine who will cover what. Better yet, request that a conference call be arranged for all of the panelists.

• If you're planning to show slides, arrange to have someone else work the lights for you. Women typically don't delegate well, but if you're busy racing back and forth to the light switch, you'll distract your audience.

• Decide what to wear well in advance of your speaking engagement, and rehearse at least once in what you'll be wearing. (See Chapter 9 for tips). Speech coaches caution against wearing anything new, since this will only add another unfamiliar dimension to the situation. Comfortable clothing should help you to feel more relaxed. The most important thing is to look professional. Unfortunately, studies show that women speakers are often judged more on the basis of style than substance. In an article for *Working Woman* magazine, Nancy K. Austin, coauthor of *A Passion for Excellence*, shares this story. "Once after giving what I thought was a perfectly good speech, a note, folded into eighths, was damply pressed into my hand by a woman from the audience on her way out. 'Do something about your hair,' it read. 'Look at Jane Pauley; if you wore your hair like hers, it would be a huge improvement.' "

• Rehearse your speech beforehand as often as you feel comfortable doing so. But don't memorize every word of it, because you will sound stiff. Also, if you get distracted and have to try to find your place, you may panic. Do, however, memorize your opening and closing remarks. Using this technique should calm your nerves and instill confidence. After delivering your first five or six lines by rote, you'll be on a roll. And if you've also memorized the last five or six lines, you can end with a well-thought-out punch.

• Use note cards, and remember that it's perfectly acceptable to refer to these during your speech. Seasoned speakers recommend printing in big letters and writing only one or two statements on each card. You can use exaggerated punctuation marks—like dashes or dots—to remind you to pause periodically. Also, consider using a colored highlighter in your notes as a reminder to maintain eye contact with your audience or as a cue to smile, use a visual aid, or use a specific gesture. Finally, consider placing your cards in a small ring notebook. That way you eliminate the risk of dropping them either on your way to the podium or while speaking.

• But never use note cards as a crutch. In fact, you should be so well prepared that you could ad-lib your speech if you had to.

• Practice projecting your voice, but refrain from shouting. Maintain a conversational style of speech, using appropriate volume and gestures to emphasize major points. To be sure that your mannerisms match your speech patterns, practice your speech in front of a mirror, a group of friends or colleagues, or have someone video-tape you as you do a dry run.

• Don't make a mad dash for the podium after you're introduced. Instead, walk in even, deliberate steps using good posture. Try to look as if speech making is something you do every day.

• Once you've reached the podium, don't start talking right away. Audiences spend thirty to sixty seconds sizing up a speaker, so take time to establish a powerful presence. Count silently to three. Adjust the microphone if necessary. Make eye contact with your audience. Smile. Count to three again. Begin.

• Audiences decide within the first ninety seconds whether or not your speech is going to be good. So never open by mumbling something like, "I'm really nervous," or "This is my first speech, so bear with me." Instead, break the ice with a good audience grabber. Ask a question. Tell a humorous or personal anecdote that relates to your topic or your audience. Share a cartoon, a startling statistic, or a provocative quote that emphasizes your theme.

• Avoid using mannerisms that spell lightweight—poor posture, looking down, playing with a pointer. In fact, avoid holding *any* props—pointers, note cards, pencils, microphones, and projector remote-control devices—while speaking. When you do, you risk fiddling with them and, as a result, distracting your audience. Also refrain from clinging to the lectern and rocking from side to side or front to back.

• Maintain eye contact with your audience throughout your speech. Some speakers have a tendency to look above the heads of their audience, which can be very distracting. Remember, studies show that people with a high degree of eye contact are judged by their associates to be more "friendly," "natural," "self-confident," and "sincere." In contrast, those with little or no eye contact are perceived as "cold," "evasive," "submissive," and "inattentive." Furthermore, when you avoid making eye contact in small-group situations or in one-on-one conversations, you may also be perceived as devious.

If you're feeling nervous while giving a speech, focusing on a friendly face in the crowd can have a calming effect. Helayne Spivak, executive creative director of Young & Rubicam, an advertising agency based in New York City, recalls one of the first speeches she gave. "I was a little nervous, but throughout my talk, there was this one face looking at me and smiling. He made it very easy for me to relax. Afterward I found the man and told him how much his smile had meant to me. It turned out that he was visiting from another country and didn't understand a word I had said!"

• When possible, *show* rather than tell by using audiovisuals to illustrate and reinforce the major points of your speech. Research indicates that audiences remember 80 percent of what they *see* and only 20 percent of what they hear. And since audiovisuals direct an audience's attention away from you, using them may help you feel more relaxed. But don't rely on them. When explaining a slide or overhead, talk to the *audience*, not the visual, and position yourself at an angle that will enable you to simultaneously address the audience and keep an eye on the screen. Turn off the projector when you're finished. Otherwise, the noise and bright light may distract your audience.

• Captivate your audience by organizing your material into lists: "Three Reasons You Should . . ."; "Five Ways To . . ."; "Top Ten Obstacles To . . ." According to Ron Hoff, author of *I Can See You Naked*, this technique is always an audience grabber. "You'll *feel* the activity in the room—bodies moving forward in their chairs, pages of notepads being flipped, papers being rustled in the search for pencils and pens," he says. "The place comes *alive*."

• Vary your pace by stopping occasionally for a "power pause." This gives your audience a chance to absorb what you've been telling them.

• If you use slides, overheads, photographs, or flip-charts, be sure they are of the highest quality. If your budget can afford it, use color illustrations, but limit yourself to one or two colors. If you're sharing statistics with your audience, make sure they are the latest figures available.

• Remember Murphy's Law, and maintain your composure when something goes wrong. A woman from Seattle wrote to Ann Landers about a large organizational banquet she'd attended where everyone was dressed in formal attire. When the chairwoman raised her baton to call the group to order, the zipper on the back of her gown broke. Unshaken, the woman finished her speech, then approached the officers in her organization and asked them to remove their name badges and pin them on the back of her dress. She then finished chairing the meeting without missing a beat. The author of this letter told Landers, "My husband, who is usually very reserved, said in a loud voice, 'Now *that's* what I call a classy lady.' "

• Close with a punch, and give your audience something to remember you by: a one-page summary of your speech, a list of resources, or suggestions for further reading.

• Above all, remember to be yourself—not some abstract notion of what you think a speaker should be. Simply talk to your audience (using power communication skills) the same way you talk to people on a one-to-one basis.

Thinking on Your Feet

Perhaps the most dreaded aspect of giving a speech is the question and answer session that follows. After all, you've had the luxury of being able to practice your speech countless times, but you can't accurately predict the questions your audience will ask. There's always that gnawing fear that someone will ask you a question that you can't answer, or worse, that someone will hassle you.

Here are some tips to help you breeze through the Q & A portion of all your presentations:

• Relax. If you know your subject matter well—and you should once you've written a speech about it—you will be able to answer most inquiries easily. And as Hoff states, "Every question you get is an indication of interest. *Welcome* it." Even if the question appears to be a hostile one, keep in mind that it still reflects interest. So don't allow yourself to become rattled.

• Review your speech and try to anticipate questions you may be asked. Or rehearse your talk in front of your family or a group of colleagues and get them to ask you questions.

• When you call on someone, point with two fingers instead of one. Nancy K. Austin, coauthor of *A Passion for Excellence*, believes, "Pointing, when women do it, usually doesn't play well. It comes across as looking accusatory. When I tried pointing with my index and middle fingers together, the response was altogether warmer. The two-finger point looks strong, sturdy, and confident."

• When possible, refer back to points you made in your speech to answer questions.

• If a question catches you off guard, take time to collect your thoughts by repeating it. Not only will the people in the back of the room appreciate this gesture, you will also be clarifying the question and giving yourself time to think about your answer.

• If you don't know the answer to a question, say so! But follow up an "I don't know" with a "But I'll find out." Then arrange to contact the questioner later with the answer, and make sure you fulfill your promise.

• If a question stumps you and there's an expert in your audience that you know can answer it, consider referring the question to her—if you've checked with her ahead of time, and she has agreed to assist you.

• Steer clear of arguments. If someone in the audience tries to criticize or badger you, stay calm. Resist the urge to raise your voice, and keep your mannerisms low-key. Acknowledge the questioner's feelings by saying something like, "I see what you mean," or "That's an interesting point." If that doesn't work, try empathy. "Pause briefly to indicate you're giving the person's thoughts serious consideration,'' recommends Stephen C. Rafe in his book *How to Be Prepared to Think on Your Feet*. ''Then say, 'You evidently have strong feelings about this' or 'I respect your views—let me give you another perspective.' Avoid using 'but' to link your thoughts, because 'but' is negative.''

If a questioner still persists, instead of saying, ''We're running out of time,'' or ''I think this is getting too involved,'' make your response positive by saying something like, ''That's a good point. I'd like to discuss it further with you during the break or after the speech.'' Then break eye contact with the questioner by searching the room to acknowledge the next inquiry.

• Be cautious of using humor to respond to a difficult question. ''A humorous acknowledgement should never be confused with a flip response that laughs away a tough question,'' says Malcolm Kushner, a California-based humor consultant and author of *The Light Touch*. ''The latter is completely inappropriate. You never want to look like you're making fun of the questioner or ignoring his concerns. A humorous acknowledgement should always be followed by a serious explanation.''

• Limit all of your answers to two to three minutes maximum. If a questioner wants more details, again, offer to meet with him one-on-one when your talk is finished.

• Avoid winding up your Q&A session by asking for one last question. This strategy can backfire if the next question is dull, negative, or one you don't know the answer to. Instead, announce, ''We have time for just a few more questions,'' then end the session on a high note—after the next good question.

• Never answer a question "off the record." As Joan Detz points out in *How to Write and Give a Speech*, there is no such thing! So never say anything you'd regret having appear on the front page of the next day's newspapers.

After you've given a speech or two, your confidence level will rise. But don't be alarmed if you still feel nervous about performing. As one well-known public figure once quipped after twenty-five years in the speech-making business, "The butterflies never go away; it's just that after a while, they begin to fly in formation."

CHAPTER 6

Mastering Meetings

"The best impromptu speeches are the ones written well in advance."

Ruth Gordon

MYTH: Most meetings are a waste of time.
FACT: Every meeting—whether you are a
participant, a presenter, or the chairperson—
represents a golden opportunity to increase
your visibility as a power communicator.

Meetings offer you an opportunity to share your ideas and demonstrate that you work well with others. They also provide you with a perfect arena to test and practice your power communication skills—listening well, speaking with confidence, using appropriate gestures and powerful body language. And don't think for a minute that superiors won't notice your imput—or lack of it. As George David Kieffer points out in *The Strategy of Meetings*, "In essence, every meeting you attend is a prospective job interview and a current job evaluation."

Successful women understand the importance of meetings

and have learned how to take advantage of them. They've also learned that you don't have to conduct a meeting to have an impact. Participants, presenters—in addition to chairpersons—can all make their presence felt.

When you are a participant . . .

How can you shine as a meeting *participant*? Here are some pointers:

• If you've been invited to attend a meeting for the first time, be prepared to introduce yourself. And don't blow an opportunity to make a good first impression by mumbling something like:

> "Gee, you caught me off guard. Let's see. My
> name is Carla, and I work in personnel.
> Actually, I'm just the gofer around the office.
> (Smile) I do a little bit of everything."

Instead, think ahead of time what you want this particular group to know about you. A more professional approach:

> "My name is Carla Jenkins. My background is
> in health administration, and I handle all of our
> company's insurance claims. It's a pleasure to be
> here."

• Familiarize yourself with the group dynamics of any new meetings you're asked to attend. Analyze the minutes of previous meetings (go back several months) to determine how decisions are usually made and who the power players are.

• Do your homework. Study the agenda, and if there isn't one, ask the chairperson what will be discussed. If handouts are distributed prior to the meeting, read them carefully. And if you have a question or need clarification on some agenda items, ask ahead of time.

• Ask if there is a special seating arrangement, formal or informal, when you attend a meeting for the first time. Lois, a training director for a hospital, says, "When I was invited to sit in on a series of management planning meetings, I kept getting vibes of hostility from one of the men. Since we'd never met, I couldn't figure out what the problem was, until my boss told me that I'd been sitting in the man's usual chair. At the next meeting, I changed seats and apologized for having taken his. He said it was no big deal, but I could tell that it was."

• If there is no set seating arrangement, sit where you can be seen and heard. Research indicates that high-status individuals select the most focal position in a group. So try to sit at, or as close as possible to, the head of the table. Or sit to the right of someone with power, and you share power. Those who occupy focal positions are also perceived as leaders. One study showed that in a group of prospective jurors, the person who takes the end seat at a table is most likely to be selected as the foreman of the jury.

If you're anticipating conflict from someone at the meeting, avoid sitting directly across from him, as this will heighten the chances for conflict. Instead, take a seat on the same side of the table several chairs away. In fact, studies suggest that if you sit on his dominant side (to his right if he is right-handed), he will feel less threatened and be more receptive to your ideas.

• Know who's who. If you're new to a group, and the chairperson asks everyone to introduce themselves, jot down names of everyone you don't know and where they are sitting. That way, when you become involved in the group's discussions, you can use people's names.

• Arrive early—not only so you can get a good seat, but so you can get to know others. This will make you feel less nervous about contributing to the group's conversations later. Also, as Kieffer points out, "Sometimes a great deal is accomplished in the few minutes before a meeting begins: people show their cards, deals are cut. You will want to be aware of this pre-meeting maneuvering."

• Don't go empty-handed. "As an attendee, you will be a valuable part of every meeting as long as you go with the intention of adding a productive edge," says Michael C. Thomsett in *The Little Black Book of Business Meetings.* "You can contribute a great deal to the purpose of the meeting by bringing something of value along: an informed opinion, important information, or a constructive idea." In fact, studies show that people who talk more in conversations with both friends and strangers are perceived as leaders. So speak up at least once during every meeting you attend. Doing this will not only increase your visibility, it lets the group know you are listening.

• Take advantage of every opportunity to make a powerful impression by preparing specific and detailed ideas for important agenda items that interest you. If, for example, you notice that "improving customer service" will be discussed, go to the meeting with a four-point plan. Since most other participants will either not speak up or will "wing it," you will stand out.

• Be ready to speak out about any controversial items on the agenda. You're more likely to be called upon to give your ideas and opinions when the group is divided on an issue. So *prepare* an impromptu speech whenever you foresee such a situation. When others *assume* you're improvising, and you've secretly prepared a speech, you'll dazzle!

• If you plan to pitch an idea, test the waters before the meeting. Approach some of the key decision makers one-on-one to see if they'll lend support to your idea. If not, consider tabling the issue until you can rework it into a more acceptable idea.

• Take credit for your ideas. What often happens at meetings is that one person's idea quickly becomes the "group's" idea. Or, frequently with women, someone else takes credit for their ideas. How can you make sure you get noticed for your input? Jane Trahey offers an excellent suggestion in her book, *Women and Power*. Whenever you go to a meeting with a new proposal or idea, summarize it in outline form on paper, and put your name at the top of the page. Make enough copies to distribute to everyone at the meeting, and lay them face down in front of you. Pitch the idea, and if it bombs, leave the papers where they are. If, however, your idea goes over well, pass them out by saying, "I've got the key points in writing. Let's build on this."

• Go the extra mile. Plan for conflict. "It might not be enough to prepare a strong case supporting your position," notes Thomsett. "If you are familiar with the issues, then you already know the opposing viewpoint. Don't simply build a case for your side; also address the arguments you know the other side will raise." Also be prepared to compromise, or to back down gracefully if the majority disagrees with your position.

• Never allow an argument to turn into a showdown. Otherwise, you'll be perceived as overly aggressive. Kieffer suggests that when you disagree with someone, it's a good idea to provide your opponent with a way to save face. You can do this by mentioning, first, any points the two of you agree on, then noting where you disagree. In other words, "share" credit of your ideas with those you are opposing.

• If you are reluctant—as many women are—to disagree with others' views for fear that you *will* appear overly aggressive, try this strategy. Say, "Let me play devil's advocate for a minute," then state your opposing view.

• Speak with authority—it's the only way to be heard. Watch those disclaimers. Don't begin a point by saying something like, "This may have already been discussed," or "Maybe this won't work but . . ." Use a moderate tone of voice with a relatively low pitch. And if you have something to contribute, don't wait too long to jump into a discussion. Research indicates that when people contribute early in a discussion, they are more likely to exert greater influence as the discussion continues.

• Use powerful mannerisms. When speaking, don't fumble around through your notes looking for information to back up your statements. If you do, you'll come across looking disorganized and are more likely to be interrupted. While listening, refrain from smiling (unless someone is saying something funny) and bobbing your head. Use power gestures instead. Look alert by sitting up straight. Show you're paying attention by maintaining eye contact with the speaker—even if he isn't looking at you. Avoid doodling, but if you think you may want to comment on what someone is saying, do jot down quick notes as others speak.

• When your presence at a meeting is viewed as controversial by some, ease into your role as an active participant slowly. Give the group some time to get used to your presence, and you'll establish credibility and gain others' trust more quickly.

Paula's story is a good example. A radiologist on the staff of a large hospital, Paula recalls, "Our department had a notoriously bad relationship with another department—which was unfortunate because we depended on each other to admit and treat patients. But most of the physicians tended to accept the infighting as 'the way it is.'

"This other department had a conference every Thursday in which they reviewed selected problem cases. Nobody in our department would attend these meetings because too many fights ensued. So, I volunteered to go every week and represent my colleagues. In preparation for each meeting, I made sure that I studied the cases to be presented ahead of time and had questions prepared to show interest. I sat in the same place every meeting—about the fourth or fifth row center—right in the speaker's line of vision and where everyone could hear me clearly should I elect to say something.

"The first couple of meetings I said nothing—even if the information presented was wrong. The next several, I asked at least one good question from the ones I had prepared. At my first opportunity thereafter, I complimented a student's presentation, but gently (and positively) added new information I'd found in the literature. Within six weeks the head of the department sat down in front of me and introduced himself. Within three or four months, every time there was a question that involved my area of expertise, the whole room would turn and look at me. And I knew I had made it when their department started asking *me* to present cases at *their* meetings. My colleagues couldn't believe it!"

> **MYTH:** Since your audience is likely to be smaller and more familiar, giving a presentation at a meeting requires less preparation than speaking at the podium before a large group.
>
> **FACT:** Giving a presentation at a meeting requires just as much—if not more—

preparation than speaking before a large and
less familiar group. In fact, making a good
presentation at a meeting will get you noticed
and can often be a steppingstone to career
advancement.

When you are speaking at a meeting . . .

Meetings are excellent training grounds for public speaking
situations. In fact, many of the same skills you've learned
to achieve credibility at the podium also apply to meeting
presentations. So keep in mind these more specific tips that
apply to making presentations at meetings:

• Your audience may be smaller, but you still need to plan
what you want to say, prepare audiovisuals and handouts
when appropriate, look *and* sound professional, and be prepared to answer questions.

• Prepare your opening and closing remarks as carefully
as you would a full-length speech. Rehearse!

• With fewer people, you can personalize your presentation
by basing it on your audience's specific interest in the topic
and by addressing their specific needs and problems.

• Use power words to pep up your presentation, particularly when you are trying to persuade your audience to buy
into an idea you have. According to research conducted at
Yale University, the most powerful words in the English
language include:

YOU	MONEY	SAVE
NEW	RESULTS	EASY
HELP	SAFETY	LOVE
DISCOVERY	PROVEN	GUARANTEE

• Brevity is a power tool, so get right to the point. Studies of managerial work time indicate that business executives spend an average of half their time in meetings. Consequently, they rank meetings as the fourth biggest time wasters. So use your time wisely and effectively.

• Use visuals to illustrate main points. Research indicates that people retain more of what they see than of what they hear. Furthermore, a study sponsored by 3M at the Wharton Center for Applied Research suggests that the use of visuals can reduce the time spent in meetings by as much as 28 percent.

• Stand while you are talking, and choose a spot where you can maintain eye contact with everyone present.

> **MYTH:** Calling and chairing a meeting will get you noticed.
> **FACT:** Calling a meeting *for a good reason* and chairing it *well* will get you noticed.

When you are chairing a meeting . . .
If you've ever attended a meeting and caught yourself daydreaming, clock watching, or squirming in your seat, more than likely the chairperson was to blame. In fact, most meetings fail for one of three reasons: they take up too much time, they involve too many people, or there is no agenda. All of these details fall under the jurisdiction of the chairperson. In other words, taking charge of a meeting requires hard work, a great deal of preparation, and assuming responsibility for specific tasks. Here are some tips to help make your turn at the helm run smoothly:

• To call or not to call a meeting. How do you decide? First, determine your goals and objectives. Next, ask yourself if these could be met just as easily by making a few telephone

Audience Turn-ons:
Words to Pep Up Your Presentations

able	help	quality
advantage	immediate	quickly
brilliant	impelling	results
confidence	instant	satisfaction
controlled	key	smart
detail	latest	solved
economical	lowest cost	special
effective	money-making	successful
emphasis	today	expert
now	top	excited
outstanding	tremendous	fair
professional	volume	

calls or by writing a memo or letter. The important thing is not to waste anyone's time. As Kieffer points out, "Holding an unnecessary meeting can undermine your reputation."

• Whom should you invite? Company policy may dictate that you invite certain people. Otherwise, everyone involved in carrying out any decisions made at the meeting should be asked to attend. Also, include key people with expertise in the areas you'll be discussing. But try to limit the number of participants, since the larger the group, the more difficult it will be to reach your goals and objectives. In fact, one way to limit the number of participants is to keep the focus of your meeting narrow. In other words, the more specific the objective, the fewer the necessary participants.

• Don't underestimate the importance of logistics—specifically the location, seating arrangement, and timing of meetings.

• **Location.** Choose an environment that is consistent with the purpose of your meeting. If, for example, your goal is to persuade others to buy into an idea you have, try to hold the meeting in your office. That way you will feel more comfortable and be better able to exert control. In your office, you also have the option of sitting behind your desk—the traditional seat of power—or making others feel more relaxed by sitting beside them. If your office is too small, a second option would be a neutral territory—like an in-house conference room—or choose a restaurant or hotel meeting room.

If the meeting is designed to brainstorm or solve problems, choose a location that is comfortable and free from distractions. Avoid choosing an oversized room, because it may *look* as if fewer people showed up than were expected. Count the number of people you expect to attend, then choose a room slightly smaller than you think you'll need. That way your meeting will have the appearance of success. A cozier atmosphere also encourages creative activity.

• **Seating arrangements.** The goals and objectives of your meeting should also play a role in the seating arrangement you choose. While most conference rooms have oblong or rectangular meeting tables, you can assert power (or chose not to do so) by controlling the seating arrangement.

According to Susan Dellinger and Barbara Deane, coauthors of *Communicating Effectively*, "If you want to appear highly *directive* in your leadership style, you will want to sit at the head of the table. On the other hand, if you want to try to *equalize* the flow of communication and encourage participants to interact with each other, you'll want to sit at a position that is off center or near the middle of the table.

"To *look* like you are being democratic while maintaining your position of leadership, take the end seat on one side of the table and seat *no one* at the head or the foot."

You can also make it a point to seat those who disagree with each other on the same side of the table a few seats away from each other. This reduces eye contact—and open confrontation—between archrivals.

• **Timing.** Meetings held late in the day or after lunch will not be as productive as those held early in the morning. Moreover, if you want a meeting to run quickly, call it at 11:00 A.M. or 4:00 P.M. Since these times are an hour before lunch and quitting time, participants will be more likely to keep their input quick and to the point.

Avoid luncheon and dinner meetings—*unless* your objective is to establish a social (as well as a business) relationship with others in attendance. Also, keep in mind that the attention span of the average person in a meeting plummets after an hour. So if your meeting stretches more than thirty minutes past that time, call a short break.

• Set an agenda. A written agenda can be your most effective power tool. It forces you to think through your objectives and encourages you to focus on strategies to achieve those goals. It tells your participants what you plan to accomplish as well as how they can prepare for the meeting. Your agenda is a script that will allow you to control the flow of the meeting. It can also serve as a tool for evaluating your performance after the meeting.

An effective meeting agenda should list all of the subjects you plan to cover, contain a brief description of each item, and include the goals you hope to accomplish for each item during the meeting. Assign a specific amount of time to each item, and prioritize the issues. A good way to jump-start a meeting is to begin with an issue you feel will be resolved quickly. Then follow this with an issue that you anticipate will take the most time, as energy tends to be highest at the start of a meeting.

Analyze your agenda to make sure your goals are reasonable. "Limit the number and kinds of tasks to be undertaken," Kieffer suggests. "The more narrow the defined task, the better the group does, and the better you will do."

When you are satisfied with your agenda, send a copy—at least a week in advance—to everyone who is expected to attend the meeting. Tell them how long the meeting will last, and let them know you are available to answer questions and clarify points about agenda items before the meeting.

• Preparation = Control. Envision the meeting. Decide what you hope will occur regarding each agenda item, and do all you can to achieve these objectives. Organize supporting materials. Anticipate questions and problems that may arise, and be ready with answers and solutions. Don't wait until a meeting to distribute important handouts. Everyone will be so busy reading them that they won't focus on the issues, and you'll waste valuable time. Doing this might also suggest that you waited until the last minute to throw something together, or it could arouse suspicion among some group members who suspect you may be trying to sneak something past them.

• Know your audience. Anticipate their attitudes on the issues you'll be discussing. Ask yourself, "What are *their* personal agendas?" Then appeal to their interests by speaking their language.

• Know your job. Presiding over a meeting involves more listening than talking. In fact, Kieffer suggests thinking of yourself as a referee or a coach rather than a quarterback. Here's a checklist to remind you of your responsibilities:

• Assign someone to take minutes. If it's standard procedure in your office for the chairperson to take notes, tape-record the meeting instead. That way you can focus all of your attention on listening and orchestrating the flow of the meeting.

• Remember, the first three to four minutes of a meeting establish its tone, so begin on a positive note. Share good-news announcements, encouraging statistics, or a humorous, personal anecdote that ties into an item on your agenda.

• Think twice before you delay a meeting to wait for late arrivals. If the majority of participants are on time, start on time—unless your boss or other important decision maker is delayed.

• Introduce each agenda item by giving a brief overview. Summarizing what action has already been taken will save time and keep discussions from backtracking.

• Brush up on the rules of parliamentary procedure, but don't be a slave to them.

• Keep the meeting moving by limiting discussion to one issue at a time. When discussions get off track and seem to be going nowhere, step in with a reminder that, "This is the issue we're discussing."

• If a subject is stalled, and everyone seems to be repeating themselves, intercede by restating the issue and summarizing any ground that has been covered. Then call for a decision. If the group can't agree on a decision, table the issue. Appoint a committee to look into the problem and proceed with your agenda.

• Define roles and responsibilities of each committee. Be sure all committee members understand what is expected of them.

• Make people feel positive and important. Acknowledge their contributions, and use their names when you do so.

• If arguments get heated and emotional, remain impartial. Separate facts from opinions. Clarify points. Get the group to focus on *how* to solve a problem, not *why* it exists. Divide big problems into smaller, more manageable ones.

• Never allow a meeting to go on once its work has been completed.

• Adjourn the meeting with an oral summary that includes all major points covered as well as any decisions made. Then recap and review any new projects assigned by naming the people responsible for each action plan, their goals and objectives, and the time frame in which they are expected to fulfill their obligations.

• Prepare a written summary after the meeting and send a copy to everyone who attended (as well as anyone who was asked to attend but was unable to be there).

• Follow up meeting assignments in writing. Make sure they are completed on time.

Above all, view meetings as your "mini-stage." Use them not only to practice your new power communication skills, but to find out what works for you and what doesn't. As Kieffer says, "Meetings are the 'window' through which you can see and evaluate your professional life—and through which you're seen and evaluated. Understanding this will make you far less casual about invitations to meet and far more demanding of the meetings you call or attend. In thinking strategically about meetings, you will become more accomplished in the art of managing people and ideas."

CHAPTER 7

The Write Track

"Writing is easy. All you do is stare at a blank sheet
of paper until drops of blood form on your forehead."
Gene Fowler

Your boss is in a rush and asks you to write a brief report
and cover letter for his signature. "Be glad to," you say. But
when you sit down to write it, do you feel an overwhelming
sense of inadequacy and a sudden desire to change jobs? If
so, you are not alone. According to Ken Macrorie, author of
Telling Writing, some 90 percent of Americans feel they can't
write. Most cite lack of confidence in their abilities and the
fear of being evaluated by their superiors as their reasons for
avoiding pencil pushing.

Lack of experience can also contribute to writing apprehen-
sion. Maybe you endured English in high school or college,
but writing was a task you hoped somehow to avoid altogether
in your career.

Then there's the monster known as grammar. The rules of
writing can be so overwhelming that you feel blocked by
pressures to do everything right. Keeping all those rules

straight in your head can be mind-boggling, and it often blocks your ability even to *begin* writing.

Yet, writing is another important way to create visibility on the job. For example, in one survey of four hundred businessmen and businesswomen, 79 percent of the respondents listed the ability to write well as an important factor in hiring employees. And since so many people fear writing, or don't do it well, mastering powerful writing skills can help you stand out in your quest to move up the company ladder.

A flair with words can lead to more powerful communication skills elsewhere—on the telephone, in group discussions, and in public speaking situations. Furthermore, good writing skills offer enormous power. You can use words to motivate, inspire, and persuade. You can also use writing to create the image you want for yourself. For example, a style that is warm, caring, and professional can enhance your image. On the flip side, a style that is aloof and superior can make you appear unapproachable.

Studies show that women are, for the most part, superior in verbal tasks—spelling, punctuation, vocabulary, and fluency. But social conditioning affects our writing in the same way it affects our speech patterns. How? Compare these memos. Can you tell which memo was written by a man, and which one was written by a woman?

To: Jane Wilson
From: Pat Smith
Date: June 13, 1992
Re: Annual Stockholders' Meeting

Thank you for your assistance in coordinating our annual stockholders' meeting last week. Your role as banquet chairman helped to make the weekend run smoothly. Your work ensured that this year's meeting was a great success.

Thank-you for a job well done.

To: Jane Wilson
From: Pat Smith
Date: June 13, 1992
Re: Annual Stockholders' Meeting

Thank you so much for your help in our annual stockholders' meeting! You were an incredible help. I especially appreciate your efforts because I know you've been so busy trying to compile the annual report. Still, it was fun, wasn't it? And the food was delicious!

Speaking of food, let's have lunch soon!

Men's and women's writing styles often differ as much as their conversational styles do. Notice, for example, the difference in tone between the two letters. The first, written by a man, is businesslike. The second, written by a woman, has a more social tone. Now consider the style and content of both letters. The message is the same, but the first example is concise and professional. The second memo, however, is filled with qualifiers, empty adverbs, and tag questions.

Some other differences typically occur in men's and women's writing. Men don't write enough; women write too much. Men tend to be more direct, while women are often reluctant to state their ideas and needs directly. And whereas men's writing is often stiff and impersonal, women are often too personal.

But powerful writing has no gender. It is direct, precise, and when appropriate, assertive. It is also concise and to the point—a one-page memo or letter gets read; a three-pager tends to get shuffled to the bottom of the pile. Powerful writers also use the active voice and write in a natural tone, using contractions and conversational English.

In fact, many of the principles of good speaking apply to good writing. Clarify your objectives. Analyze your audience. Organize your thoughts and materials. Choose the right words. The best way to get started on the right track is to answer three questions:

1. Who is my audience? One key to powerful writing is knowing who your readers are and what they want—and expect—from you. As Mark McCormack, author of *What They Still Don't Teach You at Harvard Business School*, points out, "People often overlook the importance of rank or position in determining how to communicate with others. Different people need to be communicated with in different ways. Your boss expects to be informed, your peers want to be included, your subordinates need to be instructed."

2. Why should my reader be interested? These days, everyone is inundated with written materials. Consequently, it is essential for you to tell your audience up front what's in it for them so that they will read your correspondence. For example, which of the following memos would be more likely to catch your interest?

To: The Support Staff of Quality Plastics, Inc.
From: Karen Lewis, Office Manager
Date: November 1, 1992
Re: Christmas Holidays

It is already November! Time has really flown by this year. In fact, you're probably still wondering what happened to summer!

The holidays are just around the corner—a time for families to spend time together and share in the many joys of the season. As you know, it's a tradition for Quality Plastics, Inc. to have a Christmas party every year, and this year is no exception. You'll be pleased to know that we have set the date for this year.

Mark your calendars for Monday, December 19, beginning at 4:00 p.m. More details will be sent to you later.

As an extra special Christmas present this year, our company president, Sam Jones, has announced that we have had such a productive and profitable year that he's decided to give the entire staff both the day before and the day after Christmas off.

Happy Holidays!

To: The Support Staff of Quality Plastics, Inc.
From: Karen Lewis, Office Manager
Date: November 1, 1992
Re: Christmas Party/Bonus Days Off

The date for our annual company Christmas party will be Monday, December 19th. The party will begin at 4:00 p.m.

And since 1991 has been such a productive and profitable year for the company, Mr. Jones has declared both the day before and the day after Christmas as staff holidays.

Enjoy!

Obviously, the second memo is more direct. This means it is more likely to be read and its recipients are more likely to get the information from it accurately. Another advantage to the second example is good use of the subject line. "Christmas Party/Bonus Days Off" (versus "Christmas Holidays") tips readers off right away and motivates them to read on.

3. What results do I want? If you want specific results, you have to ask for them! Women are often reluctant to do this. Instead of saying, "I need your response by May 16" they might write something like, "Please respond to this request ASAP." But if you leave it open to others' perceptions of ASAP, you risk not getting the results you want. In other words, ASAP to you might mean tomorrow, whereas ASAP to your reader might mean next week.

Once you've outlined what you want to say, write a first draft, then run a power test on your writing by checking carefully for speech patterns that can undermine your credibility. In fact, if you write on a personal computer, you can use the "search" function on your word processor to change or remove many of these elements:

• Qualifiers. Steer clear of vague words and phrases like *a great many, a number of, possibly, seems, considerably, as far as we know*, and *to some degree*.

• Intensifiers. Cross out unnecessary words like *really, so, tremendously, rather, such, quite*, and *very*, as well as tentative words like *mostly, probably*, and *generally*.

• Excessively polite language. Take out phrases like *I thought I might, I hope this*, and *I will try to*.

• Pompous language. Write to express yourself, not to impress others. Eliminate words and phrases that make you sound stiff and impersonal. Instead, use a conversational style. Pretend you're *talking* to people as opposed to writing to them. In fact, a good way to check your writing for pompous language is to read it aloud. Ask yourself, "Does this sound like me?" Also avoid using elaborate and pretentious words. As William Strunk, Jr. and E. B. White point out in their classic grammar handbook, *The Elements of Style*, ''Do not be tempted by a twenty-dollar word when there is a ten-center handy, ready and able.''

Weak Versus Powerful Words and Phrases

Instead of	Use
Per our phone conversation	As we discussed
Due to the fact that	Since or Because
Thusly	Thus
Prior to	Before
In the course of	During
In the event that/of	If
A point well taken	A good point
Enclosed please find	Here is
During the course of our meeting, we decided that . . .	We met and decided . . .
At this point in time	At this time, Now, Currently
Impact on	Affect
It is the recommendation of our president that . . .	Our president recommends
As of this date	Today
For the purpose of	For
Subsequent to	After
First and foremost	First
Along the lines of	Like
In a satisfactory manner	Satisfactorily
I am in receipt of your letter regarding	I received your letter regarding
The papers enclosed herewith require your signature.	These papers need your signature.
Call your attention to	Remind you
Attached herewith is the information you requested.	Here is the information you requested.

Instead of	Use
The reason is because	The reason is
In point of fact; As a matter of fact	In fact
My personal opinion	My opinion
For the purpose of	For
In the case of	If
Be that as it may	But
Pursuant to your request	As you requested
Honest truth	Truth
Necessary requirement	Requirement
Until such time as	Until
A total of ten	Ten
With regard to	Regarding
I am in agreement with	I agree
Absolutely necessary	Necessary

Granted, pompous language in business communications *used* to be acceptable, but the majority of today's CEOs—male and female—are avoiding stuffy writing. Instead, they use power writing skills. And power writing is short and punchy. It uses personal pronouns and short sentences. It projects sincerity, caring, and professionalism.

• Negative language. Don't start a letter with an apology or an excuse, as in "I'm sorry it has taken me so long to respond to your letter of January 10. I've been out with the flu for a week, but I'm feeling much better now." Also avoid negative words and phrases like "I regret," "You neglected," and "You should know." Instead, emphasize the positive. And if you're writing to report that you've made a mistake or to tell someone you cannot fulfill a request, stress what you *can* do, not what you cannot do.

The letter from AT&T's chairman of the board on page 74 is a good example of how to turn a negative situation into a positive one. It is also an excellent example of power writing. It uses short sentences and paragraphs. It is not overly apologetic. It comes across as caring, sincere, *and* professional.

• Clutter. Overexplain, and you risk insulting, boring, or worse, confusing your readers. Consider this example from the *Arizona Republic*:

Correction

> The Jumble puzzle, which appeared on page DI of Thursday's edition, actually was the puzzle scheduled to appear today. The Jumble originally scheduled to appear Thursday as well as the answers to Wednesday's puzzle are on page EI today. The answers to the puzzle published today appeared Thursday, and the answers to the puzzle published Thursday will appear Saturday.
>
> Source: *Red Tape Holds Up New Bridge and More Flubs from the Nation's Press* by G. Cooper/Peregrine Books NY, 1987.

Women are very detail oriented, but readers don't need a blow-by-blow description of why you are writing to them. It should be obvious. Moreover, if you wait until the end of your correspondence to ask for something you need or want, chances are, you won't get results.

Whether your correspondence is one page or ten pages, place the most important information up front. If your report exceeds two pages, include an executive summary. Statistics show that while only 50 percent of managers read full reports, 100 percent read executive summaries. Your executive summary should highlight the main points your report covers, include key results, and list overall recommendations.

Robert E. Allen
Chairman of the Board

550 Madison Avenue
New York, NY 10022
212 644-1000

Dear AT&T Customer:

AT&T had a major service disruption last Monday. We didn't live up to our own standards of quality; and we didn't live up to yours.

It's as simple as that. And that's not acceptable to us. Or to you.

Once we discovered the problem, we responded within minutes with every resource at our disposal. By late evening, normal service was restored. Ironically, the problem resulted from a glitch in software designed to provide back-up in a new signaling system we were installing to bring even greater reliability to our network. It has now been fixed.

We understand how much people have come to depend upon AT&T service, so our AT&T Bell Laboratories scientists and our network engineers are doing everything possible to guard against a recurrence.

We know there's no way to make up for the inconvenience this problem may have caused you. But in an effort to underscore how much we value our relationship with you, we've filed with the FCC to offer a special day of calling discounts on Valentine's Day, Wednesday, February 14:

Discounts all-day for residence and business customers on most out-of-state calls made on the AT&T public network throughout the U.S., and on international calls to all 158 direct-dial countries.

We've also extended the provisions of our AT&T 800 Assurance Policy to cover this extraordinary situation.

For more than 100 years, we've built our reputation on superior quality, reliability and technological innovation. Our goal is to ensure that you <u>always</u> regard us that way.

Sincerely,

R. E. Allen
Chairman

Keep sentences short—averaging between seventeen and twenty-five words. Varying the length of your sentences will make your writing flow. Limit your paragraphs to seven to eight lines maximum, because the eye needs a break at that point.

If you need to cover a lot of details, use bullets to highlight your main points. This technique, along with the use of adequate margins (at least a half-inch all around) will make your correspondence more visually appealing.

• Passive voice. The active voice packs a more powerful punch. A good way to tell the difference between active and passive voice is: in the active voice, the subject is in charge; in the passive voice, the subject is acted upon. Since you want to sound in charge, use strong words in the active voice. Here are some examples of passive (in italics) versus active voice:

The good news was enthusiastically received by the committee.
The committee enthusiastically received the good news.
A memo was sent to all new employees by the Personnel Director.
The Personnel Director sent a memo to all new employees.
The company's books were reviewed in detail by the auditor.
The auditor reviewed the company's books in detail.
Your full cooperation on this project is requested.
I appreciate your full cooperation on this project.
It is requested that your monthly report be submitted by April 18 to the Sales Department.

Please submit your monthly report by April 18 to the
Sales Department.

The papers were left on your desk by Ms. Jones.

Ms. Jones left the papers on your desk.

*Judy was encouraged by her manager to submit a
résumé for the new position.*

Judy's manager encouraged her to submit a résumé for
the new position.

*A decision must be made on this proposal ASAP to
avoid losing the account.*

We need to decide on this proposal ASAP to avoid
losing the account.

*The motion to adjourn the meeting until tomorrow
morning was made by Ellen Turner.*

Ellen Turner moved to adjourn the meeting until
tomorrow morning.

• Sloppiness. Think of your writing as a substitute for
face-to-face communication. What kind of image are you
presenting? Correspondence filled with grammatical and
spelling errors will mark you as unintelligent and unpromot-
able.

The same goes for typographical errors. Always check your
correspondence carefully—especially if someone else types
for you. And if you are responsible for typing your own
correspondence, ask a colleague to proofread everything for
you. Typographical errors are not only unprofessional, they
can also be embarrassing. For example, according to Chuck
Shepherd, John J. Kohut, and Roland Sweet, authors of *News
of the Weird*, ''The Georgia State Game Commission spent
a considerable amount of time debating the regulation of
alligator rides before someone noticed the typographical error
and realized the commission was supposed to be debating

whether to regulate alligator *hides*." Here are some other classic bloopers.

From a college flier:

"Earth Day Celebration"
Games • Workshops • Lectures
Saturday, March 16, 1991
Noon–5:00 p.m., on the Quad
Sponsored by the Ecology Department
<u>**Pubic**</u> **Invited.**

From a letter signed by the director of a public works department:

. . . Since reorganizing our department earlier this year, my staff has asked that we plan a retreat to set goals for the coming fiscal year. Your resort would be a perfect location for our meetings, and your rental agency comes highly recommended. The dates we have in mind are May 1 to 3. Do you have three adjacent <u>condoms</u> available for rent that weekend? If so, please send me information on your rates.

From a church bulletin:

The Hampton United Methodist Church will sponsor a Harvest Supper on Saturday, October 1. The dinner will be served in two seatings: one at 5 p.m. and one at 6:30 p.m. Reservations are required and may be made by contacting the church office.

The menu for the evening will be a traditional New England boiled <u>sinner</u>, rolls, homemade

apple pie, coffee, tea and cider. Admission is:
Adults $6.75, children age 6 to 11 $3.75,
children under the age of 6 are admitted free.
Source: *More Headlines* by Jay Leno/
Warner Books: NY, 1990

From a motel marquee:

COME STAY
WITH US
SPECIAL
<u>RATS</u>

Source: *More Headlines* by Jay Leno/War-
ner Books: NY, 1990

Exorcising Your Fears

Recently, Anne, a high school guidance counselor, was
asked to write an article for her state association's newsletter.
Her editor gave her four weeks to complete the article, but
after three weeks of stalling, Anne can't seem to get started
on it. "In college, I always excelled in English classes, but
I've never had any of my writing published," she says.
"What if the editor doesn't like the way I write?"

If fear of writing has you stuck, try these self-help techniques to overcome your fears:

• Don't procrastinate—it will only intensify your fears. Conquer mental blocks by starting with something easy. Write a letter to a friend, a thank-you note, or even a journal entry—anything to get the pen moving and your mind working. In fact, it's a good idea to complete a writing project ahead of your deadline so you'll have time to rewrite or have someone else critique it.

• Set the stage for inspiration. Every writer's mind feeds on different fuel, and in some instances, mood and atmosphere can be crucial to writing success. So don't despair if you need a half-dozen #2 sharpened pencils lined up in a row to get your creative juices flowing. Many a maestro has required more than that. Rudyard Kipling, for example, could only write using the blackest of inks, and Dr. Samuel Johnson demanded a purring cat, orange peel, and plenty of tea.

• Go back to basics. Skim grammar books and other introductory writing texts. Master simple sentences before going on to complex ones. Always keep a grammatical reference guide, as well as a spelling dictionary handy, and refer to these whenever you get stuck. Also keep in mind that many local colleges and universities have grammar hot lines you can call if you feel stuck.

• Can't seem to get started? Don't worry about it. Instead, time yourself to write without stopping for at least ten minutes. Ignore the urge to erase, and pay no attention to grammar, spelling, or punctuation. Once you've finished, go back and underline words and phrases that seem interesting or important.

• Organize your thoughts. Write your subject in the center of a piece of paper, then write related facts and ideas in clusters around it. You can transfer these clusters to outline form later.

• Separate tasks into writing, revising, and editing. Don't attempt to tackle all three at once. If you have time, write a draft, then put it away for a day. When you return to it for revision, read it aloud. Polish the language and grammar, then get feedback from others before writing your final draft.

• Take advantage of special writing programs or centers near you. Many employers are willing to foot the bill to improve their employees' writing skills. If there are no programs available to you, form your own group of critics.

• Above all, force yourself to practice writing. The Latin proverb preached by most writing experts is: *scribendo disces scribere* . . . which means "by writing, one learns to write."

CHAPTER 8

Lighten Up!
The Power of Humor

"Many live by their wits, but few by their wit."

Lawrence J. Peter

Have you heard the one about the woman who liked to do her housework in the nude? One morning while doing laundry, she decided to take off her clothes and toss them in the washing machine. Moments later, she noticed that the pipes overhead were leaking, so she grabbed her son's football helmet from the corner of the basement and put it on. When she heard a small cough, she turned around to find herself face to face with the meter reader. He was so bewildered that all he could manage to say was, "I hope your team wins, lady!"

Suppose the roles in this story were reversed. Would a woman, stumbling upon a nude man working in his basement, manage to come up with such a funny remark? Not according to stereotype. In fact, it has been said that women as a rule cannot tell jokes. They forget the punch line or mix up the order of events. Indeed, in her book *You Just Don't Understand: Women and Men in Conversation*, Deborah Tannen cites a study which confirms that many women laugh at jokes, but don't often remember them. Why? "Since women are not driven to seek and hold center stage in a group, they do not need a store of jokes to whip out for this purpose," Tannen suggests.

In other words, men's humor and women's humor are different. How? Barbara Mackoff, a Seattle-based, Harvard-trained psychologist, has conducted research on humor for the past six years and offers one possible explanation in her book, *What Mona Lisa Knew*. "Men's humor is like a Hollywood Friars Club roast—all playful insults and mock-hostile slapstick; while women's humor is like an episode of television's *Designing Women*—empathic and consoling, making a small comedy out of shared experiences."

But there are a host of other reasons why women are perceived as humorless—particularly in the workplace. For starters, men have been socially conditioned to use humor regularly, while women have not. Indeed, if you grew up with brothers, you can probably recall an incident or two from your childhood where if *they* told a joke about a fat lady, your parents laughed. However, if you did the same, chances are you were told, "It's not nice to make fun of others."

Since the idea that we shouldn't—or can't—tell jokes has been hammered into our heads since childhood, as adults, women tend to suppress their sense of humor. We do this mostly out of fear—that either others, particularly men, won't find our jokes funny, or that people will disapprove of our "unladylike" behavior.

But have you ever noticed how clever and downright hilarious some women are around other women; yet, in the company of men, they appear restrained and subdued? Studies confirm that women tell most of their jokes to other women, fewer to men, and very few to mixed groups. Women also prefer small audiences of one to two people and, unlike men, are hesitant to share jokes with people they don't know well.

A woman's reluctance to tell jokes may also relate to her position in the workplace. When sociologist Rose Coser looked at laughter among colleagues on the staff of a hospital, she found that there was a tendency for those of lesser authority to make fewer jokes.

Carol Deutsch, a communications consultant based in Asheville, North Carolina, suggests that some women are suspicious and cautious of humor, since so many jokes are directed at them. "Others who want to be taken seriously fear showing their humorous side will make them appear unprofessional," she adds.

Yet, humor is quickly becoming a buzzword in today's business world. In a survey by Robert Half International of vice presidents and personnel directors at one hundred of America's largest corporations, 84 percent said they thought employees with a sense of humor do a better job than those with little or no sense of humor. And in a similar survey— of CEOs—by Hodge-Cronin & Associates, Inc., 98 percent stated a preference for job candidates with a good sense of humor.

But when the CEOs polled were asked to list the qualities they felt prevented women from getting ahead, "lack of a sense of humor" was near the top of their list.

It appears, then, that a sense of humor is not only an asset in the workplace, it is a prerequisite for promotion. As Regina Barreca puts it in her book, *They Used to Call me Snow White . . . But I Drifted*, "Humor may be tolerated in lower level positions, but it will be demanded in higher ones, because humor appears as evidence of intelligence, personal strength, and quick thinking."

Besides, humor can be an extremely powerful business

tool. Not only does it foster good relationships, it bonds people together. When co-workers share inside jokes, they create a sense of solidarity among themselves.

Humor can also be motivating. Savvy managers will tell you that incorporating a sense of humor into your management style makes you appear more relaxed, confident, and approachable. It also enables your subordinates to feel more at ease. This, in turn, opens the lines to more effective communication by increasing the amount of feedback you get.

Humor has been shown to stimulate creative problem solving as well. "There is a direct relationship between ha-ha and aha!" believes Joel Goodman, Ed.D., director of The Humor Project at the Saratoga Institute, in Saratoga Springs, New York. Noting that both humor and creativity use the same skills, Goodman says, "Both draw on perspective and give us perspective. Both also help us get distance from the situation. If two people are stuck in the middle of a problem and are able to see any humor in the situation, that gives them a different perspective. Often that liberates some creativity and a new angle that they hadn't thought of. It's a lot easier to tame down an off-the-wall idea than it is to think one up originally. And research suggests that when we defer judgment that way, creativity is increased."

There is perhaps no better way to ease stress and tension than by using humor. When *Mirabella* magazine sent a reporter and photographer to the Persian Gulf to interview women soldiers at war, they found humor working overtime. For example, Air Force Captain Susan "Awesome" Angst, quipped, "U.S. Defense Secretary Dick Cheney was going to send over five thousand more Marines to reinforce the desert front lines, but he decided to send over five hundred women with premenstrual stress instead. Cheney rightly figured the women would retain water better and shoot anything that moved."

Humor has the capacity to make you part of a "club" that might otherwise exclude you. In an interview with *People* magazine, Diane English, creator of *Murphy Brown*, said, "Since the men writers outnumber the women at the start of the season, my right-hand, Korby Siamis, and I make sure we say something that shocks the men so they know they don't have to be careful around us. Then the gloves are off, and we can just write a funny show."

Still another way to use humor is in self-defense, or *akido*. Goodman explains, "*Akido* is a Japanese martial art in which the person attacked maintains his honor and dignity by turning the attack back to the attacker." This assertive (but nonaggressive) approach provides a positive way for women to hold their own when they are victimized by sexist or snide remarks.

For example, in *They Used to Call Me Snow White . . . But I Drifted*, Barreca shares the story of Liz Carpenter, former White House staff director for Lady Bird Johnson, who published a book about her experiences. When *Ruffles and Flourishes* came out, Arthur Schlesinger, Jr. remarked to Carpenter, "I liked your book, Liz. Who wrote it for you?" To which Carpenter brightly replied, "I'm glad you liked it, Arthur. Who read it to you?"

When West Point admitted their first female cadets, Betty Friedan, who was hired as a consultant, says in her book *The Second Stage*, "There was outrage, fear that women would lower the standard of courage, discipline, and physical prowess that were the ethos of West Point." Yet, the academy's first female graduates recalled the worst moments of their four years with surprisingly good humor. "Typically they would turn away obnoxious questions with a joke," Friedan says. For example, when asked, "Why are you here?" the female cadets would catch their male attackers off guard by responding, "To find a husband, of course!"

And according to Barreca, when a new co-worker asked

anchorwoman Connie Chung a fairly sensitive question about the relationship between her position as an Asian-American woman and her rapid rise in the field, Chung responded by pointing to the senior vice-president of the network and saying, "Bill likes the way I do his shirts."

Men are known for their strategic use of humor, but for most women, seizing control of an uncomfortable situation by way of a joke or snappy comeback feels risky. There's always that fear that we'll offend someone or that we'll be misunderstood. We also worry that we might be perceived as overly aggressive. Still, it's a risk worth taking, because in most instances, not only will you come across as sharp and confident, you also stand to gain credibility and the respect of others.

Besides, lightening up puts problems in perspective, helps take the fear out of making mistakes, encourages you to take risks, and helps you set and reach goals.

How can you improve *your* laugh life? Here are some expert tips that should spell comic relief at the office:

• Know the definition of humor. A falsehood many women buy into is the notion that displaying a sense of humor means being a comedienne. Mackoff offers a better definition. "It is a state of mind, an *attitude* that can be learned and practiced," she says. In others words, demonstrating that you have a sense of humor can be as simple as encouraging and reacting favorably to the mirth of those around you.

• Apply it to your working environment. Mackoff also suggests looking for ways to create inside jokes at the office, then offers a list in her book, *What Mona Lisa Knew*, of possible sources: local geography, the competition, infamous customers, cafeteria food, telephone tag, parking spaces, paperwork, length of meetings, deadlines, computer snafus, and other shared pressure points.

• Take the lead. If you're a manager, make it a point to share jokes and funny anecdotes with your subordinates. Don't worry that you may be perceived as flaky or unprofessional. In time, they'll begin to emulate you—and you should encourage that. As Victor Borge once said, "Laughter is the shortest distance between two people."

• Plan for it. According to Goodman, 95 percent of business situations can be anticipated, thus allowing you to prepare humorous solutions and responses to problems you might encounter. For example, Rick Lynch, author of *Precision Management*, once gave a speech to a group of business people. After a glowing introduction, he was handed a microphone. He tried attaching it to his lapel, but it took several tries to fasten. Meanwhile, the room vibrated with the annoying sounds of static. Next, he couldn't find his briefcase, which contained his notes. After locating it, he flipped through a few pages trying to find the section he wanted. Finally, he looked up at his audience and quipped, "How do you like it so far?"

• Rely on it to get you through the tough times. When you're feeling overworked and underpaid, or when your boss chews you out, take a five to ten minute humor break. Flip through a scrapbook of your favorite cartoons that you should compile and keep on hand for trying moments.

• Flaunt it. Hang a funny (but tasteful) poster in your office that shows others you have a sense of humor. Or, label a bulletin board in the break room "Humor Only," then invite staff members to keep it filled with their favorite cartoons, anecdotes, and quotes.

• Use it to put down pomposity. That's what Becky Klemt, an attorney in Laramie, Wyoming, did when she wrote an assertive, but hilarious letter to a fellow lawyer in California.

After winning a $4,240 child-support judgment on behalf of
one of her clients, the client's ex-husband fled to Los Angeles
without paying the judgment. Klemt sent scores of letters to
L.A. law firms in an attempt to find a California lawyer
willing to send a letter to her client's ex-husband. She received only one response—from a lawyer in Irvine, California, who wrote:

> "Without sounding pretentious, my current
> retainer fee is a flat $100,000 with an additional
> charge of $1,000 per hour. Since I specialize in
> international trade and geopolitical relations
> between the Middle East and Europe, my clientel
> [*sic*] is very unique and limited, and I am afraid
> I am unable to accept other work at this time."

To which Klemt responded:

> "Steve, I've got news—you can't say you
> charge a $100,000 retainer fee and an additional
> $1,000 an hour without sounding
> pretentious. . . . Especially when you're writing
> to someone in Laramie, Wyoming, where you're
> considered pretentious if you wear socks to
> Court. . . . Hell, Steve, all the lawyers in
> Laramie, put together, don't charge $1,000 an
> hour."

Klemt went on to "boast" about the international flavor of
her own firm by explaining that people at the firm regularly
ordered Mexican food, and that one partner had actually studied a foreign language, Latin, in high school. Then she con-
cluded:

> "Incidentally, we have advised our client of
> your hourly rate. She is willing to pay you

$1,000 per hour to collect this judgement
provided it doesn't take you more than four
seconds.''

Klemt's client never got the money from her ex, but news
of Klemt's witty letter spread throughout the legal system,
was picked up by *The Wall Street Journal*, and eventually led
to a guest appearance on *The Tonight Show*.

• Have fun with it. "Having a sense of humor is like
playing," Barreca believes. "You've got to do it, be a part
of it, to enjoy it fully." Actress Susan Lucci's attitude is an
excellent example. In the spring of 1991, Lucci, who plays
Erica Kane on *All My Children*, was passed over as best
actress for the twelfth straight year at the Eighteenth Annual
Daytime Emmy Awards. During the previous year, Lucci had
appeared in a sugar substitute commercial throwing a fake
temper tantrum over her loss. In 1991—just after the best
actress award was announced—Lucci appeared in an updated
version of the commercial in which she was shown pounding
on a desk saying, "Twelve years! What does a woman have
to do?"

But be careful to use humor appropriately. Your intent is
not to be the office clown, so don't fall into the trap of
concealing your true feelings with jokes and witticisms simply
so others will like you. As Barreca points out, "The woman
who believes that *only* by placing her experience in a comic
frame will she be acceptable, has learned to use humor in a
manner that will ultimately frustrate her, because she probably will not be taken seriously, even when she needs to be."

• Keep humor relevant to your main message. Otherwise,
it can be distracting and make you appear unprofessional.

• If you have doubts about a joke and how well it will go
over, don't tell it. And steer clear of any jokes that are based

on age, race, or sex. Otherwise, you risk offending and alie-
nating others.

• Also avoid sarcasm. *You* may think your comment is
funny, but someone else might find it negative and derisive.
A good rule of thumb to keep in mind when trying to decide
the difference between constructive and destructive humor
is: With *constructive* humor, you laugh *with* others; with
destructive humor, you laugh *at* others.

• Never joke about sensitive subjects—the firing of an
employee, an impending takeover, the loss of an important
account. If you do, others may resent you for trivializing such
serious issues.

• When you use humor as a means of self-defense, do it
nonchalantly, via your speech patterns and body language.
"It has to appear not to matter to you at all," says Barreca.
"Otherwise, it won't work."

• Above all, eliminate self-deprecating humor from your
agenda. Comediennes like Joan Rivers and Phyllis Diller may
be applauded for putting themselves down, but when other
working women engage in self-deprecating humor, they not
only reinforce negative stereotypes, they risk being taken
literally. Besides, as Barreca points out, "Your wit should
give evidence of your strength, not of your vulnerability."
   However, occasionally poking fun at ourselves can help us
gain control of a situation as well as the respect of others. At
the 1986 symposium on "Humor and the Presidency" for
example, former President Gerald R. Ford delighted his audience by giving demonstrations of clumsiness, a trait he was
perhaps best known for. He leaned unsteadily on a podium
and nearly fell. He introduced his former press secretary, Ron
Nessen, as "Don." Later, during a break, he also stumbled

into a serving tray of dishes, insisting that he did it deliberately as a joke.

Deborah Norville's story, as told by Mackoff in *What Mona Lisa Knew*, is another good example. "When Norville replaced the popular Jane Pauley as co-anchor on NBC's *Today Show*, NBC staffers dubbed her the "stewardess" because of her perky manner," Mackoff writes. "Norville responded to the unflattering nickname by dressing the part at a writers' meeting. She playfully mirrored their insult—and gained their goodwill—by wearing a blue jacket, blue pants, white shirt, and a wings pin, serving them coffee from a beverage cart."

You Can Give It,
But Can You Take It?

Studies of children show that girls usually appreciate cartoons and jokes just as much as boys do. Yet, females appear to be more influenced than males by whether or not *other* people are smiling and laughing. If they are, women are likely to join in with gusto. If they aren't, the tendency is to censor laughter with a taut smile or a token giggle.

Yet, women lose out on the many benefits of humor when they stifle a deep, hearty laugh in reaction to something that is meant to be funny. And by flashing a weak smile instead, they fail to seize a perfect opportunity to connect with others, as well as a chance to demonstrate a strong sense of self-confidence.

Besides, laughter is more genuine than a smile—particularly for women. "The glazed smile is generic; the laugh is specific," Barreca notes. "The smile is passive—not so much a statement as an expected reply. A smile is also ambiguous—

no one knows for sure what's behind it. But when a woman laughs out loud, everyone around her knows how she feels.''

Men and women also *react* differently when they are the targets of jokes or insults. Typically, men who are teased take it in stride and join in the laughter. This good-natured attitude signals to others that the "victim" has a strong self-image. Women, however, tend to take teasing personally. They may turn red with embarrassment, or they may react with anger. With either response, everyone involved is left feeling awkward.

When the joke's on you, how can you maintain perspective and control of your emotions? Use *akido* by making a joke in response. That way you invite a person to laugh *with* you.

The same strategy can be equally effective when someone tells an offensive joke in your presence. Oftentimes, a man will do this in front of a woman deliberately—it's a test to see how she will react. And according to Barreca, a woman has three options: to be humorless and sour-faced, to be a pushover by giggling, or to show him that you are someone who fights humor *with* humor.

The choice is yours.

CHAPTER 9

Strategic Listening

"Learn to listen. Opportunity could be knocking at
your door very softly."

Frank Tyger

While hosting an office reception, your boss introduces
you to the newest member of your firm's board of directors.
You shake hands with him, then strike up a conversation.
The two of you are trading ski vacation stories, when a colleague walks over to join the discussion. "I don't believe
we've met," the board member says, reading your mind. But
as you begin to introduce them, the board member's name
completely escapes you.

Forgetting names is just one symptom of poor listening
skills. Others run the gamut from daydreaming to inter-
rupting. Poor listeners are those who look over your shoulder
in search of someone or something more interesting, as well
as those who listen to you with scowls on their faces, or
worse, blank stares.

Powerful communicators are strategic listeners. They know
that effective communication in business means not only
knowing how to express themselves but also how to listen

and draw people out. They know that by listening to someone, they are communicating an important message to that person: "Your thoughts and opinions matter to me. You are worth my time." Powerful communicators recognize that listening is an active, not a passive, skill and that effective listening involves four phases:

- hearing the message
- interpreting the message
- evaluating the message
- responding to the message

They are also aware that good listening can reduce tensions, provide important information, win friends, help solve problems, and improve job performance.

The problem is, not many of us—men *or* women—are powerful listeners. Fortunately, this is a skill that can be mastered with practice and an awareness of the obstacles that prevent us from listening effectively. In fact, research shows that most of us use only one-fourth of our listening capacity.

Here are the most common types of poor listeners. See if you can recognize your shortcomings:

Pencil and paper pushers. Do you take notes when you listen? If you do, you risk becoming so involved in the physical act of writing that you only half-listen. Try tossing the pad and pen. Focus, instead, on the speaker. You may be surprised at how much more you retain.

- **Eager beavers.** Some listeners become so eager to jump into a conversation that they interrupt speakers, often finishing their sentences for them. Studies show that men do this more often than women do. But since nobody likes to be interrupted, show respect for speakers by refraining from second-guessing what they are trying to say.

• **Turned off, tuned out.** Are there certain people you dread having to listen to? Maybe they talk too slowly. Perhaps their New York accent turns you off. Or maybe they're wearing too much cologne or perfume. When prejudices like these are present, you're less likely to listen objectively to what people are saying. And they may very well be trying to tell you something important!

• **Daydreamers.** Studies show that people talk at a rate of 125 to 150 words per minute. However, we can listen at a rate of 600 words per minute. Great, you say! I can listen four times faster than people talk! What happens, though, is that many of us use this excess time to take mental excursions. The next time you find your mind wandering when someone is talking to you, reestablish good eye contact—it should jolt you back to listening more effectively.

• **Selective listeners.** When people tell us something we don't want to hear—or express an opposing viewpoint— many of us slip into a selective listening mode. We either tune speakers out or we become so busy planning our response to their ideas that we don't hear what they are saying. Instead, we should hear them out, because through attentive listening, we may discover important information that may alter our opinions. Besides, selective listening can make us defensive, when we need not be.

• **Distracted listeners.** Nearby sights and sounds—traffic, telephones, copy machines—can easily prevent us from focusing on what a speaker is saying. When someone wants to talk to you, close your office door—or find another private setting. This not only ensures confidentiality but also signals to the speaker that you really care about what he has to say.

• **Emotional deafness.** Say a colleague comes to you and starts talking about your boss. If you and the boss have recently had a disagreement, chances are you will tune the speaker out. But suppose your colleague is telling you that the boss is considering you for a special assignment. Chances are, you'll miss the message because you aren't listening.

Studies show that we forget about half of what we hear within eight hours and that eventually we forget 95 percent of what we've heard unless cued by something later on. How can you sharpen your listening skills? Try these tips:

• Don't try to remember all of what a person is saying. Go after ideas. Listen for main points and supporting facts, forgetting any unnecessary details. When a person is finished speaking, summarize what she has been saying to make sure you heard correctly.

• Use body language to *look* like an effective listener. Convey a positive and encouraging attitude by facing your speaker. Lean forward slightly to indicate, "I'm open to what you're saying." Nod occasionally to show you are listening. Maintain good eye contact. Ignore and eliminate distractions. Avoid tapping your foot, biting your lip, gazing out the window, and looking at your watch. These mannerisms send the message, "I have more important things to do than listen to you."

• Listen for *content* as well as *intent*. According to Gloria Hoffman and Pauline Graivier, coauthors of *Speak the Language of Success*, at least half of what we say every day is misunderstood or misinterpreted. So try to identify your speaker's purpose. Does she need help solving a problem? Does she want to share information? Does she simply want to blow off steam? When you know what your speaker's intent is, you can listen in more appropriate ways.

• Listen between the lines. Take note of a speaker's body language. For example, changes in voice, tone, and volume may have meaning. So may someone's facial expressions, posture, hand gestures, and body movements. Women are better than men at reading body language, so use this skill to your advantage. Listen with your ears *and* your eyes.

• Don't interrupt—unless a person is going too fast, or you need to clarify a point. Many of us have a bad habit of finishing others' sentences. Oftentimes, we do this to show off or because we think we're paying a compliment to someone. But instead, we risk offending the speaker or coming across as arrogant and self-centered.

• Be flexible. Keep an open mind by mentally categorizing what others are telling you as *ideas*, not facts.

• Focus on content versus delivery when you are listening to someone who doesn't express herself well.

• When trying to solicit others' ideas, and they don't seem willing to talk, put them at ease by finding common areas of interest to discuss first. This may help to draw them out; then, they will feel more comfortable sharing their opinions and suggestions.

• If someone makes a suggestion you dislike or expresses an opinion you totally disagree with, hold your fire. Granted, this is no easy task. As Nancy Austin, coauthor of *A Passion for Excellence*, points out in an article for *Working Woman* magazine, "Making room for opinions other than our own is heroic work. Everyone knows that even a teeny complaint has a half-life of about 50 years for the person on the receiving end. Compliments, according to a similar law of physics, vaporize in 30 seconds flat." In addition, if you attack others, you will be viewed as argumentative or contentious.

• Avoid offering advice unless it is solicited. Don't interrupt the speaker with unnecessary comments and questions.
Powerful listeners will tell you that by letting others talk
something through, they often find their own answers. Responding appropriately also means rephrasing, in your own
words, what a speaker has said to confirm that her message
has been heard.

• Follow up listening with a speedy response. When people
make suggestions, and you promise to "look into them," you
are obligated to fulfill that promise as quickly as possible.
Take a minute to write quick thank-you notes to those who
share ideas worth investigating. Then keep them posted regarding how their suggestions may or may not be used.

• Listen aggressively. Austin suggests, "When you want
to know what's on your staff's minds, listening is better when
done in *their* territory. Keep it casual, and realize that you
will have to make roving listening a habit before anybody
truly believes you are serious about it. Go without a note pad
and clipboard, and if in your travels, someone comes up with
a nifty idea you want to remember, ask to borrow her pen
and note pad."

• When you are interrupted by something else pressing,
apologize to the person you're listening to and set a time
when the two of you can resume your conversation. This tells
your speaker, "What you have to say is important to me, and
I want to give it my full attention."

• Use empathy. "Mirroring" a speaker can help you build
trust and establish rapport. Mirroring entails matching the
tone, rate, and volume of your voice to those of the speaker.
It also involves noticing and using some of the same words,
gestures, and phrases that she does. Mirroring a speaker can

break down barriers and help you find common ground. This, in turn, results in more effective communication. The trick, of course, is to do this without being obvious, so focus on *approximating* a speaker's oral and body language rather than imitating him.

• Listen for others' "hotbuttons" and use them to your advantage. Hoffman and Graivier define hotbuttons as "areas of passion and sensitivity—things we know will elicit a certain response from someone in a given situation." Hit a negative one, and you turn someone off. Find a positive one, appeal to it, and you'll likely find success.

• Learn to tolerate silence. A short pause in conversation is not necessarily a cue for you to take up where a speaker left off. Rather, silence can have a variety of meanings. It may indicate that your speaker doesn't understand what you've said. It may mean she needs a moment to digest and contemplate your words. Or, it could mean that she'd rather not say anything, because she has nothing constructive *to* say. It may be a sign that she is feeling dumbstruck or emotional about what you've said and doesn't trust herself to talk. Whatever the reason, you should learn to keep mum and use silence as a power tool.

Unfortunately, few women do this, because we don't understand silence. It intimidates us, and we become so uncomfortable with it that we typically rush in and say anything to avoid it. Yet, according to Hoffman and Graivier, when you break the silence first, you have lost control. "So don't do it—even though a minute of silence can seem like an eternity," they advise.

In fact, you should learn to use "power pauses" to your advantage. "Being quiet is actually a very mature aspect of good verbal communication," Hoffman and Graivier add.

"But although it sounds quite logical, people tend not to do it. Instead, they insist on filling up the silence. That, however, is precisely what makes silence such a powerful tool for those who have the control to use it: other people will want to fill the gap of silence when you don't. It becomes a question of who blinks first!''

For example, when Patricia, a lab technician, went for a job interview, the employer was so impressed with her presence and credentials that he nearly offered her the job on the spot. "I got home from work and found a message on my machine," she says. "I waited until the next morning to call him back, and he made an offer on the telephone. The salary he proposed was much more than I was making at the time, but rather than show my excitement, I paused to give the impression that I was thinking it over. Then just as I was about to accept his offer, he rushed in and made me an even higher one!''

- Remember that listening doesn't mean agreeing with someone. It does, however, mean giving your undivided attention to what others are saying. That way you gain credibility and respect. You also mark yourself as an effective leader. Indeed, powerful managers have learned that there is genuinely no higher form of flattery than listening to someone.

On the other hand, there's nothing quite so unnerving as bearing your soul to someone, then realizing that they haven't been listening. For example, in an interview in *Reader's Digest*, Carol Burnett shares this story about a conversation with her seven-year-old daughter after a spanking.

"At bedtime, she was still sniffling. So I went in and put my arms around her saying, 'Now, you know I love you very much.' And then I talked about character and what she did that was wrong, and she listened—never taking her eyes from my face. I began congratulating myself—boy you are really getting through, she'll remember this when she's forty.

I talked for twenty minutes. She was spellbound; we were practically nose to nose. As I paused, searching for the clincher, she asked, 'Mommy, how many teeth do you have?' ''

CHAPTER 10

First Impressions

"Nothing succeeds like the appearance of success."
Christopher Leach

Four minutes. Studies tell us that's the amount of time we have to make an impression upon someone we've just met. And within a mere ten seconds, that person will begin to make judgments about our sense of professionalism, social class, morals, and intelligence. What happens is that people tend to focus, first, on what they see (dress, appearance, eye contact, movement). Next, they focus on what they hear (rate of speech, tone and volume of voice, articulation). Finally, they focus on our actual words.

Furthermore, first impressions are often lasting ones. Which means that when you play your cards right, you can enjoy the benefits of what sociologists call the "halo effect." In other words, if you're viewed positively within those critical four minutes, the person you've just met will likely assume that *everything* you do is positive.

Unfortunately, however, the reverse is also true. Boggle a first encounter with someone, and in most cases, that person will mistakenly assume that you have a slew of other negative traits and characteristics. Worse, the person is not likely to take the time or make the effort to reformulate a second or third impression of you.

Maria's story is a good example. Maria has spent the past six years working nights while attending college during the day. "I've always wanted to be a teacher," she says, "and I worked hard to earn my degree. When I finally graduated, I was very optimistic, because there were several positions open." In fact, Maria had her eye on a teaching position at an elementary school a few blocks away from her apartment. "I knew several of the teachers there, so I thought my chances were good," she says. With the help of her friends at the school, Maria landed an interview. But it didn't go well. "I was running late that morning and noticed on my way out the door that I had a tiny run in my stockings," she recalls. "I thought about changing, but I knew I'd be late if I did. By the time I got to the interview, the run had stretched from my ankle to my knee. I walked into the interview and immediately apologized to the principal for not looking my best. Then I spent most of the rest of the interview trying to sit and stand in such a way that he couldn't see the run."

Maria was not offered the job; in fact, one of her friends told her that the principal's only comment about the interview was, "If a person doesn't take the time to present her best image at an interview, what kind of teacher is she going to be?"

In short, most employers believe that those who look and act as if they care about themselves are more likely to care about their jobs. What can you do to take advantage of the halo-effect philosophy and avoid becoming the victim in a case of mistaken identity? Your goal is to come across as physically attractive. Not beautiful, not even pretty—but attractive. In the way you dress, in the way you move, in your

facial expressions, in the gestures you use, and in the way
you speak.

We know that it's what's inside that counts, but research
shows that physically attractive people are generally perceived as more intelligent, likable, and credible. In fact,
studies show that even juries are swayed by physical attractiveness. Defendants who are perceived as physically attractive tend to receive less severe punishments.

Fair or not, it's a fact of business life. How can you present
your most attractive self?

Dressing For Success

Let's focus first on wardrobe. Clothing and accessories tell
us a lot about people. Dress well, and you signal success,
power, positive habits, and high status. Studies have also
linked clothing consciousness to higher self-esteem and job
satisfaction. In fact, one study funded by Clairol Corporation
found that it pays, literally, to dress for success. Judith Waters, Ph.D., a professor at Farleigh Dickinson University,
sent out "before" and "after" photographs with identical
résumés to over one thousand companies and asked them to
determine a starting salary for each of the "candidates."
(None of the companies received both "before" and "after"
photos.) The results? Companies indicated an initial salary of
8 to 20 percent higher for those whose images had been
upgraded!

Yet, many women fail to comprehend the importance of
dressing for success. Consider Natasha's story, for example.

Natasha has worked for ten years as an administrative assistant in a large accounting firm. She is dedicated, dependable,
and extremely competent. Whenever the office manager is
out sick or takes a vacation, Natasha fills in. But when the

office manager retired last year, and Natasha applied for the position, she was not even granted an interview. "I thought it was an oversight, so I asked the director of personnel what happened," she says. "He told me that I didn't fit the image they were looking for in an office manager. He then suggested that I revamp my wardrobe—by getting rid of all my neon-colored skirts and dangling earrings—and try again for another position. I was shocked. I do a great job, and the way I dress shouldn't have any bearing. My clothes reflect my personal style."

Betty Harragan, author of *Games Mother Never Taught You*, says, "There is no question in my mind that many women are held back in their job progress because of their inattention to dress. Forget expressing your personal taste. Your clothes must convey the message that you are competent, self-confident, reliable, and authoritative."

How can you dress for success? Here are some points to remember:

• Dress for the job you *want*, not the job you have. Take note of what the person whose position you aspire to wears, and dress in a similar way.

• Avoid heavy and flashy make-up—especially brightly colored eye shadow, lipstick, and blush-on. Save false eyelashes for weekend wear.

• Steer clear of anything that spells "little girl"—ruffles, bows, fabrics with cute prints, brightly colored hose, penny loafers or "Mary Jane" type shoes, and hair ribbons or "cutesy" barrettes.

• Never wear anything seductive or clingy to the office. This includes see-through blouses, low-cut dresses, and skirts with high slits.

• Wear a tailored jacket to signal authority.

• Make sure all of your clothes fit correctly.

• Suits are great, but become optional at higher levels. According to Gilda Carle, Ph.D., a communications consultant in Yonkers, New York, "Women starting out in business should wear suits to command respect. However, executive women or decision makers can safely wear dresses to complement their power image." In other words, the higher up you go, the more you can break the rules.

• Ties are taboo for all women.

• Wear shoes you can walk in—no extremely high heels.

• Jewelry is fine, but the simpler the better. Avoid anything that dangles, shines, or makes a lot of noise.

• Don't carry both a handbag and a briefcase to a meeting or interview, because clutter makes you appear low status. Keep in mind that bulky briefcases send the same message, since subordinates usually attend to more paperwork. Finally, always carry a briefcase in your left hand, so your right hand will be free for handshakes.

• Build your wardrobe around safe solid colors. A few pieces with small, subdued prints will work, but stay away from bold, colorful prints. Also keep in mind that white or gray can make you look washed out.

According to Carle, safe power colors are navy and shades of it. What about red and black? "Keep in mind that red can be overpowering," she says. "It's best to wear it if you're already accepted by your audience, or if you're giving a keynote speech where you want to stand out. Black can be stark, so use a pale blouse or dynamic accessories to soften the effect."

• When appropriate, dress down to avoid outshining someone important. If, for instance, your manager is hosting a reception and tells you she's decided to wear a casual suit and accessories, don't show up dressed to the nines.

• Dress to suit specific occasions as well. If you're giving a presentation to your company's board of directors, wear your most professional-looking outfit. If you're having lunch at a construction site with a group of carpenters, dress casual.

• Always keep a spare pair of hose in your desk drawer in case yours run. Also, have on hand a small make-up case filled with the essentials needed for a quick touch-up.

• If you have an interview at a company you've never visited and aren't sure what to wear, drop by ahead of time to investigate their dress code. Or, send for a copy of their annual report and study what those in power are wearing.

• Consider tapping the resources of a personal shopper. Once a luxury for the likes of the Ivana Trumps and Princess Dianas of the world, today personal shoppers are catering more and more to the nine-to-fivers. Offered by most of the better department stores, personal shoppers can provide you with the clothes you need, at the price you want, in usually under two hours, and at no charge for their services. By looking at the kind of business you are in, your age, figure, coloring, and personal style, they can keep you from making costly mistakes. Since building the right office look requires skill—and personal shoppers have the know-how—why not get pampered a bit?

The Body Connection

Of course, first impressions—and physical attractiveness—are dependent on more than just the way you dress.

Remember the Mehrabian formula: 7 percent of any message comes from the words we use, 38 percent comes from our voice, and 55 percent comes from our body language. Applied here, it means that when you're getting the once-over from someone, you will be judged more, at least initially, by the body language you use than by the words you say.

This principle explains why oftentimes when you've just met someone, the person will say something a few moments later like, "What did you say your name was?" or "I'm sorry, where do you work?" Generally, the other person is so busy sizing up and interpreting the way you are communicating nonverbally, that she hasn't been listening to what you've been saying.

Here are some pointers to help make your first encounters positive ones:

• Always greet people you've never met before with a firm handshake. If they don't initiate the gesture, offer your hand first—even when they are female.

• Smile when you shake hands, then maintain a neutral expression while you continue talking. Of course, if the person says something humorous, feel free to laugh and even respond with an appropriate witticism of your own.

• When going for a job interview, don't enter talking. It can make you appear nervous or unsure of yourself. If you have a choice of seats, choose a chair beside the interviewer's desk as opposed to one across from him. That way there are no barriers between the two of you. And if you have to sit across the desk, shift your chair slightly so that you're not directly in front of him.

• Monitor your body language to make sure you don't come across as desperate for the job or as too eager to please. Look comfortable. Act as if you're enjoying yourself.

Say What You Mean, and
Mean What You Say

In first encounters, the person you've just met will eventually get around to analyzing your speech patterns. This is the time to clinch that favorable first impression. How? By making your voice and choice of words *consistent* with your body language and appearance. If they aren't in sync, you send out mixed messages that are bound to confuse your audience. If there is a discrepancy between your words and body language, your body language will be believed.

Your goal? To exude confidence. How?

• Open and close your conversation with a positive remark. In an interview situation, for example, you might tell the interviewer how much you've looked forward to meeting her. If you've studied the company's annual report (and you should have!), consider remarking on any substantial progress the firm has made within the last year, or cite an area of company involvement that interests you. When you leave the interview, summarize why you are the best candidate for the job and thank the person for her interest.

• Ask questions. Too often when people meet for the first time, there is an awkwardness about what to say after the introductions are over with. Yet, most people love to be asked questions, so be the initiator. Then focus on being a powerful listener.

• Master the art of small talk. Most people who *appear* comfortable with strangers in social and business situations will tell you that they've worked hard to look that way. Their advice? Read at least one daily newspaper (especially the sports section) and weekly news magazine so that you can hold your own in almost any conversation.

• When trying for a new job, blow your own horn! Highlight your abilities and accomplishments. List and summarize problems you've solved in your present position as well as any positive results you've achieved. Use power phrases like, *"In my present position, I've increased company sales by x amount of dollars,"* *"Here's a list of the projects I've undertaken in the last year, and here are the results,"* and *"Here are some of the professional problems I've encountered in the past two years, and here's how I solved them."* Don't worry about sounding conceited. This is what an interviewer expects to hear!

Material Things

Your working environment can also affect people's impressions of you. For example, last year Katherine and Jackie, both interviewers in the personnel office of a large university, competed against one another for a promotion. "It was a tough decision to make, because they were both so competent," recalls Susan, their personnel director. "They were also both hired at about the same time, so neither one had seniority." Who got the promotion? Jackie. Why? "I hate to admit this, because it sounds trivial, but Katherine's office is always in such a disarray that we decided to choose Jackie," Susan says.

This reasoning goes back to the rationale that employees who take care of themselves (and their working environment) are perceived as caring more about their work. So make it a point to keep your office or work space reasonably neat.

If you're fortunate enough to have an office of your own, decorate it to project the image you want others to have of you. A few plants and one or two family photographs add a nice personal touch, but don't clutter your office with an overabundance of knickknacks, family pictures, and souvenirs from recent trips, as these can make you appear "fluffy." Be careful about displaying any religious symbols as well. You don't want to risk offending anyone, and your office isn't the proper place to demonstrate your religious preferences. Also, think twice about placing a candy jar on your desk, as this tends to invite co-workers to stay and chitchat.

Instead, fill your walls with work-related charts and graphs, photographs of projects you've completed, reprints of articles you've been featured in, and certificates or citations you've received in your profession.

In other words, your office should *not* look like your living room at home. You do not want to look too permanent, because you're on your way up! And once you reach the top, you can make your own rules.

How You Look On Paper

Finally, make sure your résumé also reflects the image you want to project. Your focus should be on your achievements, and the best way to accomplish this is by using the active voice. For example, instead of saying, "Responsible for development and implementation of several cost-saving measures," say, "Developed and implemented several cost-saving measures." And instead of boasting, "Demonstrated skill in customizing seminars to target company's needs," say, "Customized seminars to target company's needs."

Update your résumé regularly, and keep it current by eliminating all jobs you held ten years ago or more. Check your references before you list them as sources to contact, and have your résumé typeset or laser-printed. Keep it short (one to two pages) and target each résumé to the specific job you are going for.

Take the example of Kate, who worked as an office manager and administrative assistant for seven years before deciding to change careers. Eager to find work as a travel consultant, Kate sent her original résumé to several agencies. When she didn't land a single interview, she realized the need to become more specific in showcasing her credentials.

Kate's theory proved correct. After submitting her revised résumé (see her "After" example), Kate landed a job in her chosen field almost immediately.

Before and After: Which Résumé Got the Job and Why?

What makes Kate Newton's "After" résumé better?

• She dropped the name Kathryn, choosing to use only the name she goes by. Using more than one name on a résumé can undermine your sense of professionalism and confuse your reader.

• She eliminated the vital statistics section (date of birth, height, weight, and marital status) altogether. Sharing this information on a résumé gives interviewers an opportunity to prejudge you before ever meeting you!

• Kate tightened her career objective to make it tailor-made for the position she was applying for. When your objective is vague (as in Kate's "Before" résumé), your résumé will likely end up in the slush pile. So focus on writing your objective as if the job description was written specifically *for* you!

• Kate's new résumé captures an interviewer's attention by listing her strongest assets up front.

KATHRYN ("KATE") NEWTON

175 Dearing St.
Franklin, MI 48025
(313) 851-7218

Date of Birth: 8/10/60
Height: 5'6"
Weight: 128
Marital Status: Married,
 two children (in school)

OBJECTIVE: Seek challenging position with well-established and growing company with opportunities for advancement and good fringe benefits.

EDUCATION: Melrose High School, Melrose, MA
Member of Beta Club and Volleyball team

Miami University, Oxford, OH
Graduated in 1982, 3.19 GPA
B.A. Degree in French

Kankakee Community College, Kankakee, IL
Psychology Courses

EXPERIENCE:

June 1987–
Present:
OFFICE MANAGER/SALES SECRETARY, Allen Industries, Highland Park, MI. Responsible for all paperwork and data processing for this one-girl front office.

October 1985–
January 1987:
SALES DEPARTMENT ADMINISTRATIVE ASSISTANT, El Chico Imports, Miami, FL. Responsible for record-keeping and follow-up for Sales Manager and staff.

June 1985–
September 1985:
SWIM INSTRUCTOR, Green Acres Country Club, Cincinnati, OH. Took this part-time summer job as we were preparing to move and needed to help with household details.

September 1982–
April 1985:
TRANSLATOR/OFFICE CLERK, Le Jeune Products, Cincinnati, OH. Translated correspondence and in-person communications for French firm. Helped out with clerical work as needed.

May 1983–
September 1984:
WAITRESS, Days Inn of America, Miami, OH. Part-time job to help pay way through college.

HOBBIES: Swimming, hang-gliding, travel, and chess.

BEST PERSONAL AND PROFESSIONAL REFERENCES
UPON REQUEST

More Power to You!

KATE NEWTON

175 Dearing St.
Franklin, MI 48025

Telephone: (313) 851-7218

OBJECTIVE: Position as Travel Consultant . . . especially where a strong sales background and organizational skills are needed to get the job done!

Personal Characteristics: Self-starter . . . highly motivated . . . effective telephone skills . . . computer experience . . . resourceful . . . ability to learn and assimilate new information quickly.

EDUCATION: B.A. Degree in French; Minor in Spanish, 1982. Miami University, Oxford, OH.

Languages: Fluent in French and Spanish.

EXPERIENCE: **SALES AND CUSTOMER SERVICE**
Over 7 years administrative experience working in Sales. Deal extensively with customers over the phone, developing skill in problem solving. Assisted Sales Manager in creating training program in Customer Relations. Sales increased by 30% and customer retention rate doubled, after first year of program.

BROAD TRAVEL BACKGROUND
Have traveled extensively throughout Europe, Asia, and Northern Africa. Have planned detailed itineraries for trips, both domestic and abroad. Fluent in French and Spanish, with conversational ability in German and Dutch. As Translator for Le Jeune Products, a Paris-based firm, traveled widely with corporate officers throughout the U.S. and France.

COMPUTER AND ORGANIZATIONAL SKILLS
Four years' experience working on MS/DOS. Handle customer billing and accounting systems for office. Compile monthly newsletter, using Pagemaker 4.0.

PROFESSIONAL HISTORY: OFFICE MANAGER, Allen Industries, Highland Park, MI 1987–present.

ADMINISTRATIVE ASSISTANT, El Chico Imports, Miami, FL 1985–87.

TRANSLATOR, Le Jeune Products, Cincinnati, OH 1982–1985.

• In the Education section, Kate eliminated all old and irrelevant information. For example, since she had a college degree, there was no need to list where and when she graduated from high school. She dropped her Beta Club and Volleyball team memberships, as they dated her. (Note: It's okay to list noteworthy high school achievements, but *only* if you've graduated within the last five years. Otherwise, it looks as if you're trying to pad your résumé.)

Kate also chose not to highlight courses she'd taken at a community college in the updated version of her résumé, because they did not pertain to the job she wanted. She decided, instead, to highlight noteworthy *skills* that she possessed as the *result* of her education (see Languages in the "After" example).

• Since Kate was changing careers, she opted to use a format different than the standard chronological résumé. In an effort to showcase her skills and assets (versus a chronological list of where she worked and the duties she was responsible for in the "Before" example), she organized her new résumé into experience categories. She then chose subheadings (Sales and Customer Service, Broad Travel Background, Computer and Organizational Skills) designed to pique an interviewer's interest.

• In her new résumé. Kate deleted any jobs she'd held that didn't pertain to the position she was seeking—like Swim Instructor and Waitress. She then analyzed her employment history for skills that were relevant to her new objective—like Translator and Sales. She also eliminated any mention of why she'd left a position (as in "took this part-time job as we were preparing to move . . ." in the "Before" example). If a potential employer wants to know why you left a position, she will ask.

• Kate decided to take out the hobbies section when she revised her résumé, since swimming, hang-gliding, and chess did not relate to the position she sought. As a rule of thumb, include hobbies on your résumé *only* if they relate specifically to your objective or enhance your qualifications. Otherwise, they may rob you of credibility.

• Finally, Kate eliminated the heading Best Personal And Professional References Upon Request. After all, what interviewer *wouldn't* expect her to provide her best references, and how often do interviewers ask for personal references? Besides, if an interviewer wants to contact your references, he will ask for them.

Whether you're presenting yourself on paper or in person, always put your best foot forward. Take advantage of those crucial first four minutes of every first encounter by exuding attractiveness. Look high status, move with confidence, speak with conviction, and the halo effect can be yours!

CHAPTER II

Telephone Power

"Is this the party to whom I am speaking?"
Lily Tomlin

The very instrument that was supposed to be the greatest timesaver in our history has turned into the biggest timewaster. The telephone causes more interruption and generates more stress than anything else in our business environment.

Yet, the telephone can be your most powerful business tool. How? It provides you with an opportunity to make a positive first impression of both yourself and your organization. Think of the many times you've used the telephone to call a company for information or service. If you've never visited the operation in person, your perceptions of its competency and efficiency were based entirely on how its personnel handled your call.

With the telephone, you can accomplish twice as much in half the time. The telephone can also help you get noticed. As Jean H. Klein points out in *The Phone Book*, "Being knowledgeable about your organization and conveying that knowledge courteously on the telephone is a way to impress your supervisors with your professional competency.''

But the rules for communicating by telephone are different than they are for face-to-face conversations. In person, we're granted four minutes to make a good impression; on the telephone, we have only *seven seconds*! Furthermore, because we are deprived of using body language, gestures, and facial expressions on the telephone, Mehrabian's formula no longer applies. In other words, we can no longer rely on nonverbal clues (55 percent) to provide meaning to our communication. We can't nod to indicate understanding. We can't greet someone with a firm handshake. We can't make eye contact to develop rapport. As a result, it's much easier to be misunderstood over the telephone.

On the flip side, however, there are advantages to communicating by telephone. When we don't have to worry so much about how we're dressed or if we'll be considered attractive, we're better able to focus all of our energies on what we want to *say*. By the same token, the fact that others *can't* read our body language or see what we look like prevents them from being influenced by their own prejudices in making judgments about us.

In fact, on the telephone, we have the capacity to project whatever image we want. Carolyn, for example, who runs a successful résumé service out of her home, says, 'I've learned to project the image of a three-piece-suit professional while wearing a warm-up suit!''

It's often easier to deal with angry people over the phone than it is in person. You can concentrate better on what they're saying when you can't see the daggers in their eyes.

Dr. Gary S. Goodman, author of *You Can Sell Anything By Telephone*!, believes it's easier to close a deal over the phone than it is in person. ''When we attach a great amount of ceremony to closing a deal, we make the matter seem very grave, and the buyer senses that there is a great deal of tension riding on his or her decision,'' he explains. ''When we ask for a yes or no by telephone, it seems to be a much more simple matter, and we find that prospects are more inclined to take a plunge without the second-guessing that enters into sit-down meetings with us.''

Several studies also indicate that the telephone offers definite advantages for certain kinds of negotiations. For example, laboratory studies in both Britain and the U.S. suggest that it's easier to change others' attitudes on the phone than it is in person.

Furthermore, your chances of being deceived and manipulated are less on the telephone. Why? In face-to-face negotiations, speakers can often use nonverbal cues to control the impressions they make on you. They can also monitor your reactions and adjust their nonverbal messages accordingly. Of course, both of these strategies are impossible to carry out over the telephone.

In fact, establishing power communication skills on the telephone requires us to cultivate a whole new set of cues to indicate our feelings and make good impressions. And to fill that missing link from Mehrabian's formula, we can rely only on our tone of voice and choice of words.

What's Your Telephone IQ?

Without visual clues, callers will find verbal ones to judge you by. So the trick is to use the seven seconds you have wisely. Here are some tips to help you do that, as well as learn how to use the telephone as an instrument of influence and power:

• Answer promptly. Oftentimes, business is lost simply because of an unanswered phone. The ideal time to pick up the receiver? Between the second and third ring. Granted, in a busy office, it can be difficult to get to the phone by the third ring, but studies show that if you don't answer by the fifth ring, callers begin to form a negative image of your organization. After five rings, they will assume that the staff is inefficient, uncaring, and indifferent to their concerns. After six rings, most callers give up. And if they don't, when you answer, you will have lost your seven seconds to make a good impression! Consequently, the caller will perceive both you and your organization negatively even *before* the phone is answered.

If at all possible, avoid answering a call by immediately asking, "Can you hold?" and never leave a caller on hold for longer than one minute without checking back to see if the caller would rather leave a message.

• Sound like a pro. Different positions require different openings on the phone. *If you are the receptionist*, and must deal with a large volume of calls, you need only greet the caller and identify the company, as in, "Good morning, Acme Industries." If you can spare an extra two seconds, tag your ID with, "How may I direct your call?" It gives you a strong professional finish.

If you are a staff member, and your calls are routed to you through the switchboard, identify your department and yourself, as in, "Sales Department, Janet Jones." To assume control, add, "How may I help you?"

If you are an executive, and your calls are screened, you may answer only with your name, as in, "This is Joanne Dailey," or simply, "Joanne Dailey." But make sure you don't come off sounding brusque or abrupt. Keep the pitch low and slow to inspire confidence and trust.

If you sound like a pro, callers will perceive you as such. In most types of communication, callers tend to mirror the conversational style of the other person. Consequently, if you project an intelligent I-know-what-I'm-doing attitude, people will assume you do, and that will be their frame of reference for interacting with you. If, on the other hand, you project stress and vulnerability, that's how the other person will respond to you.

• Answer with enthusiasm. Every time you answer the phone, your (and your company's) image is on the line. So sound positive and upbeat. Smile. Your caller may not be able to *see* your smile, but they will *hear* it in your voice. Besides, when you project cheerfulness and enthusiasm, callers will pay more attention and be more cooperative.

• Personalize your phone calls by asking for—and using—the caller's name. Some people don't like to be called by their first name, unless they know you well, so address a man as Mr. and a woman as Ms. This gives the caller the option of saying, "Please call me John," or "Please call me Mary."

Calling a person by name not only shows that you care, it tells others that their call is important to you. When callers sense that, they will trust you. And the objective of *every* call is to build trust, for only then can you begin to use the telephone as an instrument of influence and power.

Using a caller's name is a form of flattery as well. As Dale Carnegie once said, "There's no sweeter sound in the English language than the sound of your own name."

When you use a person's name periodically in a conversation, they will pay more attention to what you say. This, in turn, increases the likelihood of getting the results you want. It also allows you to interrupt the caller without asking for permission or appearing rude. Here's an example: "Ms. Rogers, I'd like to make sure you get the correct information. Please let me transfer you to our bookkeeping department.''

This technique can also be used as a subtle means to regain control over a nonstop talker. When people hear their names spoken, they instinctively stop talking.

• Communicate with confidence. Watch those qualifiers, as they can be just as damaging—if not more so—on the telephone as they are in person. Overuse them, and callers will perceive you as weak and lacking credibility. Examples include *possibly, kinda, sorta*, and *perhaps*.

Using good posture on the telephone can also help you project confidence. Callers may not be able to *see* whether you are slumped over in your chair or sitting erect, but they will be able to detect the difference in your voice.

• Don't treat a phone call as an interruption—even when it is. Granted, taking a call when you're busy with another project can be annoying. But to the caller, it is *not* an interruption, and you give up power and lose someone's trust when you appear to be indifferent or irritated.

If you are working under a tight deadline and really can't spare the time to talk, take a moment to acknowledge the call with warmth and sincerity. "It's good to hear from you, Jane!" or "Thanks for returning my call, Jane!" are good examples. Then explain briefly why you can't talk at that moment, and arrange a time to return the call.

Otherwise, accept the interruption, and remember that you are obligated to give the caller the same complete attention that you would if she were in your office.

• Screen and transfer calls professionally and efficiently. *Never* follow up a "Who's calling?" with an immediate, "Oh, I'm sorry, he just stepped out." If the person is out, the time to say so is *before* you ask for the caller's name. And never make a caller repeat a long and complicated message to you before saying, "I'm sorry, but we don't handle that. I'll have to transfer you."

When you transfer a call, give callers the full name of the person you are transferring them to as well as the department and extension or direct number. That way, if callers need to call back, they will know how to reach someone directly and won't have to waste your time.

• When a call is for someone who is out of the office or unavailable, be careful how you share that information with the caller. Avoid phrases like, "She's not in yet," "She's still at lunch," "We haven't heard from him," "We don't know *where* he is," and "She's not around." Also refrain from giving out personal information, as in, "She had an appointment with her gynecologist this morning," "He's home with the flu," or "She's here, but she's got an awful migraine."

In an article for *The Wall Street Journal*, James T. Bowers shares this story:

> "The secretary of one manager I know told a caller that her boss had gone on vacation. 'Oh,' replied the caller, 'where did he go?'
>
> 'Disney World,' said the secretary. 'He'll be back a week from Monday. Is there a message?'
>
> 'No thanks, I'll call back in a couple of weeks.' As it turned out, he did more than call back; he paid a personal visit to the vacationing boss's house and made off with several thousand dollars' worth of stereo and television equipment."

• Take a complete message. Make it a point to get as much information from callers as possible. You can do this by first asking for the full name of the caller and his organization. If you're not sure how to spell a name, ask! Second, get his telephone number, including the area code. Next, ask if he'd like to leave a specific message, and if it's a lengthy one, read it back to him when he's finished giving it to you. Wrap the conversation up on a friendly note by saying something like, "Thank-you for calling, Mr. Jordan. I'll make sure Ms. Brown gets your message." Finally, note the time and date you took the message along with your initials, in case the recipient has questions.

• Offer to help. If you're privy to most of what goes on in your organization, instead of taking a message, offer, "How may I help you?" The caller will be grateful if he doesn't have to wait until someone else returns his call. And if it turns out that you can't help him, offer to get the answer for him, and call him back as soon as you get it. This gesture will not only please the caller, it will also impress him (and your supervisors).

• Use powerful listening skills. Poor listening skills are the number-one cause of miscommunication on the telephone. In fact, nothing frustrates and irritates callers more than feeling as if they are talking to a wall. So turn away from your other work and concentrate on what your caller is saying. Don't interrupt—except to confirm facts and opinions or to clarify a point you missed. Do show you're listening, however, by periodically using comments like, "Yes," "I see," "Uh-huh," and "Go on." These will encourage your caller to keep talking. Besides, silence on the telephone can easily be misinterpreted as a sign of indifference or that you are distracted.

If you *are* distracted by someone else while you're on the telephone, ask the caller to excuse you for a moment. Tell the person who's distracted you that you will get back to her when you're finished. Then apologize to the caller for the interruption, and continue your conversation.

Take notes about what the caller says, then *prove* you've been listening by repeating and summarizing the highlights of your conversation. This will reassure the caller that his message has been heard. Also, summarize important phone calls in writing for your files. Otherwise, you may forget important details.

• Use positive language. In the absence of nonverbal cues, your choice of words on the telephone becomes even more important than in face-to-face conversations. So make sure yours pack a positive punch by downplaying the negative. For example, compare these two responses to a customer's request:

"We're absolutely swamped. I can't possibly have that out until Friday morning."
"I'll get right on it and have it out to you first thing Friday morning."

The upshot is the same—the package will be shipped Friday morning. But one way the client thinks he's getting a raw deal; the other way, he thinks you're really on the ball and that you're operating in his best interest. In other words, he now thinks he's getting a good deal!

A cardinal rule of customer service: Don't tell people what you *can't* do; tell them what you *can* do. It all has to do with your phrasing and the way you frame the situation for them. And as Nancy Friedman, president of the St. Louis, Missouri–based consulting company, The Telephone Doctor, points out, "It doesn't take any extra time to be nice."

In fact, eight years ago, Friedman was so put off by the negative telephone treatment she received by her insurance company that she threatened to cancel her policies and take her business elsewhere. Her agent responded by inviting Friedman to talk to his company's staff about how they could improve their telephone skills. The reaction to Friedman's impromptu presentation was so positive that she started her own telephone consulting company.

Today Friedman conducts workshops and seminars on the topic. Her advice? Learn these "five forbidden phrases," and banish them from all of your telephone conversations:

Forbidden	A better approach
1. I don't know.	1. Let me check for you.
2. We don't (or can't) do that.	2. Let me see what I can do.
3. You'll have to call or write....	3. Here's how we handle that. Please call or write....
4. Hang on a second; I'll be right back ...	4. I'll need to put you on hold for a minute. Is that all right?
5. No.	

Besides, courtesy pays. According to a study by the Rockefeller Institute, 68 percent of a company's client base lost each year is due to indifferent or negative phone treatment. Note that the business wasn't lost due to poor quality or competition. It was lost because of the perception on the part of the caller of indifference or lack of caring.

To help you get in the habit of using positive phrases, take this quick quiz.

The Caller's Perception:
Using the Positive Approach

Here are some examples of commonly used negative telephone phrases. Pretend you're the caller, and try to figure out what's negative about each statement. Then rewrite each one into a positive statement. (To check your statements, turn the page for explanations and a list of replacements.)

1. Afternoon, Acme Industries. Gail here.
2. I'm sorry I can't help you. I work in sales. You should have called someone in our service department.
3. I'll be honest with you. I'm really not too sure how long the warranty is on that equipment.
4. I'll be happy to find out that information for you, but I can't get to it until tomorrow morning.
5. Sounds like we made a mistake. Let me transfer you to our manager of shipping. I'm sure he can help you resolve the problem.
6. I can understand why you're so upset, Mr. Jones, but please don't take it out on me.
7. I'm sorry to keep you waiting, but things have been crazy here all week.
8. I don't have that information. I'm just the receptionist.
9. I'm going to speak with our public relations director regarding your question. If I can find out the answer from her, I'll get back to you.
10. I'm going to have to transfer you to Mr. Peabody. But this is a new phone system, so don't be surprised if you get disconnected.
11. We're short staffed this month and can't ship your order until June 20. Will that do, or would you rather cancel?

12. You have to pay your current balance before you can order anything else.

Wouldn't you rather hear . . .

1. Too informal. Instead, try: *Good afternoon, Acme Industries. This is Gail speaking. How may I help you?*

2. Who's sorry now? The customer! Especially since he has no idea who to call in service! A better way: *Joe Green in our service department has that information. Would you like me to transfer you, or may I have him call you back?*

3. Customers don't appreciate this kind of honesty. If you're not sure, offer to find out. A better response would be: *I don't have that information at my fingertips, but I can find out and call you back within an hour.*

4. This statement is positive for the most part; however "but" adds a negative slant. A better approach: *I'll be happy to find that information out for you, and I can get it to you first thing tomorrow morning.*

5. Again, almost positive, but replacing "problem" with "issue" makes it 100 percent positive: *Sounds like we made a mistake. Let me transfer you to our manager of shipping. I'm sure he can help you resolve the issue.*

6. Avoid words like "upset"; show you care and that you're listening: *I can understand why you feel as you do, Mr. Jones. You're saying that . . .*

7. The first half is positive, but the second half is not. A better response would be: *I'm sorry to keep you waiting. How may I help you?*

8. Don't underestimate your importance. If you convey

that you are *just* the receptionist, that's how you will be treated. Instead: *I'm the receptionist, and don't have that information. I'm sure Ms. Baxter can help you. Let me transfer you.*

9. The first sentence is positive, but everything goes downhill from there. The "if" is negative and tentative, and the caller is left in limbo wondering if a call will ever be returned. A better approach: *When I confirm the answer to your question, I'll call you back. What's your deadline for this information?*

10. Saying "have to" sounds like someone is holding a gun to your head! Show them you know your stuff with: *Let me transfer you to Mr. Peabody in marketing, who has that information. For future reference, his direct number is . . .*

11. Never give a customer an open invitation to take his business elsewhere. A better approach: *We can ship your order promptly on June 20. Thank-you for your business.*

12. An easy way to reframe this situation in a positive way: *Once you pay your current balance, we'll be happy to fill your next order immediately.*

• Know how to hang up on long-winded conversationalists. Many women have been socially conditioned to believe that it's the *caller's* responsibility to end a conversation. But the rules of propriety have changed. No longer must you waste time feeling frustrated because you can't get a caller to hang up. It's perfectly acceptable for *you* to take the initiative.

How can you do this politely and professionally? Start speaking in the past tense ("I've *enjoyed* talking to you," or "I'm so glad you *called*"). Discuss any action you plan to take ("Let me look into this and get back to you first thing tomorrow"). Or, show appreciation ("Thank-you for calling").

• Handle irate callers with finesse. When a caller is frustrated and angry, there's a tendency to take it personally. You may even rationalize that you're going to lose the caller's business anyway, and try to get even by snapping back. Don't!

According to George R. Walther, author of *Phone Power*, studies show that when a complaint is resolved, the caller is six times as likely to become a long-term customer.

The best way to deal with angry callers is to combine all the telephone power skills you've learned thus far. Sound positive, concerned, and eager to help. Take notes. Don't interrupt, but let callers know you are listening by using their names periodically as well as statements like, "Uh-huh," "I see," and "Go on." Both of these strategies should have a calming effect.

Indicate that you've taken notes by summarizing what you've written, then verify that you have a good understanding of the situation. Ask them what you (or your company) can do to appease them. "Sometimes all they want is an apology or an attentive audience," Walther points out. Use positive language to convey a solution. Finally, end the conversation by confirming what you've agreed upon, and follow up on any promises you make.

Power Plays on the Telephone

Thus far, we've discussed strategies to use when you are the *recipient* of a call. Here are some additional tips to increase your power communication skills when you are the *initiator*:

• Take control. Control is determined at the beginning of every phone call. Typically, the *caller* is in the position of control, so whenever possible, try to be the caller. That way, your mind-set is focused, your notes are in front of you, and you are mentally prepared for the call.

How can you assume control when you are not the caller? Ask the first question. For example, answer your phone by saying, "Sales Department, Sally Wilson. How may I help you?"

Note the subtle difference between "May I help you?" and "*How* may I help you?" The latter is much stronger. It implies that you can help the caller; it's simply a matter of "how?"

• Plan for your calls. Make the telephone work *for* you by treating each call just as you would a face-to-face meeting. Draft an agenda. Set objectives. Outline what you want to say. Determine the best time to make the call. Be prepared to answer any questions the caller may have by anticipating questions and gathering all relevant information (files, records) you may need *before* you make the call. In short, know where you want the call to go. Take charge!

• Be prepared to leave a message—with a receptionist, secretary, or an answering machine. Many people say they loathe answering machines and refuse to deal with them. However, they are a fact of life in the Information Age, and by refusing to deal with them, you'll lose valuable time.

• Avoid playing telephone Ping-Pong. Studies indicate that the average businessperson wastes five to seven hours a week playing telephone tag. You can avoid this by scheduling a specific time for call-backs.

• When trying to get through to a busy person, exude confidence. Act powerful, and the human obstacles that are standing between you and the busy person you're trying to reach will assume you *are* powerful. They will also be more likely to help you. So instead of using negative language on someone's secretary ("He's probably not in," or "I assume Mr. Frank is still in a meeting"), identify yourself, and tell the person exactly why you're calling. If you still can't get through, thank the secretary for her help and ask her to pinpoint a better time for you to reach her boss.

• Go for the halo effect by presenting a favorable first impression to someone you've never spoken to before. This can be trickier on the telephone than in person. Remember, taking advantage of the halo effect in face-to-face encounters depends on being perceived as attractive in the way you dress, move, and talk. Translated to the telephone, your *voice* must come across as attractive. You can do this by combining a warm and friendly tone with positive language.

Of course, you can master all of these strategies and still come off looking unprofessional if you don't know how the telephone hardware system works. For example, when the president of Marcia's company began putting together a team to examine the feasibility of moving to new and larger headquarters, she was tapped to be a team member. "I was surprised, because I'd been here less than a year," Marcia says. "But my boss said he chose me because I have a knack for details. He'd noticed that I was one of the few employees in the entire company who'd taken the time to figure out our sophisticated telephone system."

CHAPTER 12

Management Style

"Because of their age-long training in human relations—for that is what feminine intuition really is—women have a special contribution to make to any group enterprise."

Margaret Mead

Sensitive. Cooperative. Caring. Thoughtful. The negative effects of social conditioning on women? On the contrary, management gurus are saying that these characteristics are fast becoming necessities for business success in the nineties!

For example, in *What They Don't Teach You At Harvard Business School*, Mark H. McCormack suggests that traditionally feminine management styles translate into sound business practices.

Throughout their best-seller, *In Search of Excellence*, Tom Peters and Bob Waterman cite many examples where participative management styles increase employment involvement, and where positive reinforcement has led to higher profits for a number of American companies.

In a survey of male Fortune 500 company CEOs, a substantial percentage credited executive women with bringing a humanizing quality to the corporate world, as well as with improving business.

In an article in *Nation's Business*, Edward M. Moldt, managing director of the Snider Entrepreneurial Center at the Wharton School of the University of Pennsylvania, says that women's management styles are "right for the times." Today's companies need leaders who are "strong enough people that they're capable of hearing the ideas of others, really empowering them to use some of those ideas in changing businesses and in making them successful."

And in *Megatrends 2000: Ten New Directions for the 1990s*, authors John Naisbitt and Patricia Aburdene write, "To be a leader in business today, it is no longer an advantage to have been socialized as a male. Although we do not fully realize it yet, men and women are on an equal playing field in corporate America. Women may even hold a slight advantage since they need not 'unlearn' old authoritarian behavior to run their departments or companies."

So the good news is that many of the characteristics corporate executives are deeming critical for future success are the very traits women have been reared on. As a result, there has never been a better time for women to break into management.

However, some of these very traits, when carried to the extreme, can be our undoing. Consider these stereotypes of women in management:

• The **shrink** is overly sympathetic. Got a problem? Her office door is always open. And while her willingness to listen is admirable, her superiors and colleagues can't help but wonder how she finds time to manage work that must be done.

• The **social worker** puts everyone else's needs ahead of her own. Often emotional, she takes empathy overboard. She can't seem to make decisions on her own; instead, she seeks others' opinions before setting or changing any policy or procedure.

• The **saint** will do anything to avoid conflict. In fact, she goes out of her way to avoid confrontation and, consequently, spends too much time trying to unruffle feathers.

• The **mother hen** interferes, overinstructs, gives unsolicited advice, fosters dependence, and takes things personally.

• The **cheerleader** is cute, bubbly, and always cheerful. She dresses in ruffles and bows, organizes most of the office's parties, gives lots of compliments, and agrees with everyone—always.

• The **iron maiden** is rigid and always serious. She rarely speaks of her personal life and is critical, aggressive, cold, and competitive.

• The **daughter/kid sister** is fun and easy to talk to but appears vulnerable. Men have a paternal attitude toward her and tend to overprotect her. But they don't take her seriously.

• **Superwoman** must do everything for herself. She demands perfection from herself as well as others. She also has a tendency to overextend herself by taking on multiple commitments and roles. She rarely asks for support, yet resents it when nobody offers it.

Many of these traits have the potential to be positive. But these women have failed to create a balance between their "humanizing" qualities and a sense of professionalism. How can you make these traits work *for* you?

For starters, keep in mind that, as Deborah Tannen, Ph.D., author of *You Just Don't Understand: Women and Men in Conversation*, points out, women's inclination to seek agreement can be extremely advantageous. They're more inclined to consult others and involve employees in decision making. In turn, when employees feel they've played a part in setting policies, they're more likely to implement them willingly and efficiently.

Yet, to be powerful, managers must still possess the ability and conviction to make decisions on their own.

In fact, when the Center for Creative Leadership asked senior executives of Fortune-100-size companies to describe two female executives they knew personally—one they considered a success and another they thought had the potential for success, but who did not make it—one factor mentioned frequently as a prerequisite for success was the ability to make decisions.

Empathy—within limits—can also be beneficial. Once viewed as a distinctive disadvantage in business, it's now seen as a potential resource. In negotiations, for example, it's crucial for management to understand what the other side wants, and an empathic and perceptive manager can be a valuable asset in such situations. But when managers carry empathy to the extreme—by spending too much time building consensus and going out of their way to avoid conflict—they give up power.

Sensitivity and unselfishness are also valuable managerial qualities—until a manager begins putting everyone else's needs ahead of her own.

Since women traditionally use language to create connections and establish intimacy, as managers, they often have a difficult time working with people they don't like. Men, on the other hand, don't like everyone they work with either, but they cope. As Gilda Carle, a communications consultant based in Yonkers, New York, notes, "Haven't you seen two men who can't stand each other slapping one another on the back after they clinch a deal? Men learn to do this by playing team sports, where the object is to move the ball and score. And to accomplish this, the captain doesn't pick players who are friends, but rather, those who each bring a special skill to the team.'' In other words, powerful managers understand that you don't have to like someone to get a job done.

Then there are women managers who mistakenly equate powerfulness with ruthlessness. They want total control of their employees and try to maintain it by constantly criticizing and checking up on them. They rarely delegate important tasks and refuse to include their staff in making decisions. They attempt to motivate others with fear and intimidation.

Studies have confirmed that female managers who try to appear tough and macho—like stereotypical males—are negatively perceived. In the Center for Creative Leadership study, for example, derailment factors most often mentioned by the executives surveyed were: "She tried too hard to be one of the boys. She tried to act macho, rode roughshod over people."

Studies also show that women managers who conform to stereotypically *female* management styles are also negatively perceived. Executives participating in the Center for Creative Leadership study said of women who didn't succeed as managers, "She's a giggler. She comes across as a little girl. She loses presence power."

Is this a no-win situation? No. The answer lies in adopting a management style that is powerful, yet genderless. A style that encompasses all the power communication skills you've mastered thus far—mannerisms, speech patterns, body language, voice, and listening skills. Studying this review chart should help you pinpoint your strengths—and weaknesses.

Management Styles

Powerless	Powerful	Overpowering
Wishy-washy	Flexible	Inflexible
Unassertive	Firm	Ruthless

Powerless	Powerful	Overpowering
Puts rights and needs of others ahead of self	Respects rights and needs of others	Ignores rights and needs of others
Avoids giving criticism	Gives positive criticism	Overly critical
Avoids confrontation	Confronts when necessary	Looks for reasons to confront
Modest, passive	Confident, frank	Conceited
Superpolite speech; profusely apologizes even when not to blame	Direct and concise; apologizes when wrong but not for thoughts, opinions	Insensitive; never apologizes or admits blame
Doormat; accepts blame even when not wrong	Speaks up when she is wronged	Accuses others of wrongdoing even when she is to blame
Puts self down	Sells self	Oversells self
Doesn't take credit	Accepts credit and shares with staff	Never shares credit with staff
Smiles too often, giggles, nods	Smiles when appropriate	Rarely smiles or laughs
Uses distracting gestures, slumped posture, poor eye contact, eyes frequently look down	Uses powerful gestures, good posture, good eye contact	Uses overpowering gestures, hands on hips, stares

Research suggests that people prefer powerful *leaders*, not necessarily those who are male or female. And most negative qualities associated with female stereotypes—taking things too personally, overly concerned with petty details, too emotional, lacking clout, and so on—are not the result of sex differences. Rather, they describe the feelings and behavior of powerless *people*. People in token positions. People stuck in dead-end jobs. People in powerless *positions*.

Consequently, once women are perceived as power communicators, not only will many of the negative female stereotypes be shattered, but women in management will have more and more opportunities to shine. Furthermore, the shift in our nation's economy is quickly moving from a manufacturing base to a service and information base. In addition, many corporations are replacing their hierarchical structures with a team-approach management style that the Japanese have been so successful at incorporating.

Both trends require managers with strong interpersonal skills. Both call for leaders who have a knack for motivating employees. And best of all, both place women at a distinct advantage.

CHAPTER 13

The Politics of Communication

"A woman has to be twice as good as a man to go half as far."

Fannie Hurst

Joan had been working as an assistant vice-president in a large manufacturing firm for six years when her office manager, a senior vice-president, resigned. "Because of my seniority—plus the fact that I'd filled in for my boss whenever he'd been traveling, out sick, or on vacation—I felt confident about being promoted," Joan says. "But my hopes were dashed the day before my interview, when a co-worker told me she'd heard that the selection committee was leaning towards hiring a male colleague of mine who'd been with the firm less than two years."

Joan spent the night before her interview trying to determine the best way to sell herself for the position. "But I was so nervous that I couldn't think straight," she says. "So I asked my husband for advice."

Joan's husband, Rob, a senior vice-president at a large credit bureau, offered, "Be aggressive, and let them know you're in the driver's seat. Charge into that interview like the job is already yours. Tell them you're overqualified for your present position, and threaten to resign if you don't get the promotion. That's what I'd do.''

Joan laughed in response to her husband's "pep talk." "You're telling me to act like a man," she said. "I can't do that.''

It used to be that many women who broke through the so-called glass ceiling did so by emulating men. But women are changing. For example, in her landmark survey of 465 executives, Judy B. Rosener found that "now a second wave of women is making it into top management, not by adopting the style and habits of men, but by drawing on skills and attitudes they developed from their shared experiences as women.''

Furthermore, women have gained a new sense of pride in themselves. In 1946, when a Roper poll asked women, "If you could be born again, would you prefer to be male or female?'' 25 percent said male. Yet, when *New Woman* magazine posed the same question to six hundred women in 1990, only 6 percent said they'd rather be men.

In fact, according to the *New Woman* survey, Americans appear to be in the midst of a "gender evolution," and almost nobody wants to turn back the clock.

That includes men—who are also changing. Surveys show that a majority of today's men value qualities like "personal growth," "self-fulfillment," "love," and "family life," over "getting ahead" and "making money."

Benjamin Spock revised his phenomenally popular parents' guide, *Baby and Child Care*, to include the pronoun *she* when referring to children. "The main reason for this revision is to eliminate the sexist biases of the sort that help to create and perpetuate discrimination against girls and women," he wrote. "In discussing the clothes and playthings parents buy their children and the chores they assign them, I took it for granted that there should be a deliberate distinction between boys and girls. But this early childhood differentiation begins in a small way the discriminatory sex stereotyping that ends up in women so often getting the humdrum, subordinate, poorly paid jobs in most industries and professions and being treated as the second-class sex.''

Even some of the most powerful men in America are shattering male stereotypes. In June of 1991 while delivering a speech to the Southern Baptist Convention in Atlanta, President George Bush shed a few tears when discussing the Persian Gulf Crisis. "I feel very strongly about those kids who gave their lives for this country," he told reporters. "So if I show some emotion, that's just the way I am."

And one of the most popular adjectives used by reporters to describe General H. "Stormin' " Norman Schwarzkopf is "caring." For example, in the *Los Angeles Times*, columnist Ellen Goodman notes, "This complicated character seems to synthesize conflicting and changing male images. Introspective, but decisive, caring yet competent, one of the guys and a leader? Not stuff that always comes in the same male package."

As their role models are changing, so too, are today's children. For example, studies indicate that working mothers provide role models associated with competence and status. Other aspects of the employed mother family—the involvement of the father, the greater participation of children in household responsibilities, and more egalitarian sex-role attitudes—have also been linked to greater self-confidence and competence in girls.

As a result of the players changing, the game is evolving as well. Stereotypes are dissolving—albeit slowly in some instances—and progress is evident in many arenas.

For example, on the plus side, advertisers are beginning to notice the economic potential of women and are treating them with more respect. On television commercials and in print ads, the number of females depicted as doctors, scientists, and executives is increasing. An occasional ad might even show a man washing dishes or folding laundry.

Children's picture books and textbooks have been updated to include more girls and women and to show the latter in more progressive roles. And on college campuses, innovative programs designed to bridge the gender gap are enjoying phenomenal success.

For example, in the Leader's Program, sponsored by the National Institute for Leadership Development, women are taught to be aware of strengths they already have and to do skill-building work in new areas. Participants in this program attend intensive seven-day workshops, then select innovative projects to complete on their respective campuses with the help of a mentor (often a man). In the past decade, more than two thousand women from all fifty states and some foreign countries have gone through the Leader's Program. Participants have initiated more than 1,500 projects on community college campuses throughout the U.S. And statistics, averaged over the past ten years, show an overall 75 percent job promotion rate for females who have participated in the program!

In 1991, the Leader's Program introduced a new five-day workshop that calls for colleges to send both male and female leaders to participate. Lecturers present information that heightens awareness of gender-based leadership styles and issues, then focus on building teams that honor those styles. After the workshop, each pair is expected to return to their campus and provide similar training for their colleagues.

Many major corporations are following suit. Companies like DuPont, NYNEX, PepsiCo, and Lotus Development Corporation have instituted programs designed to help employees understand gender differences.

According to Regina Barreca, author of *They Used to Call Me Snow White . . . But I Drifted*, women are beginning to be perceived as more humorous. "Over the last few years, women have made a real change in shaping the profile of public humor," she says. "Women have found in comediennes like Carol Leifer, Joy Behar, Susie Essman, Elayne Boosler, and Rita Rudner a mirror to familiar experiences, comedy that reflects the feminine perspective."

In the political arena, women's potential for political clout is enormous. According to the U.S. Census Bureau, not only do female voters outnumber males (63.4 million versus 55.1 million registered voters in 1988), women vote more often than men. In the last presidential election, for example, nearly seven million more women than men went to the polls. Consequently, candidates and political parties are beginning to slant their campaigns—and agendas—to women voters.

According to *New Woman*'s poll—which surveyed 600 women and 601 men—traditional concepts of masculinity and femininity are nearly extinct. When asked to choose qualities they admired most in men and women, traits for both the "ideal man" and the "ideal woman" included "caring/nurturing," "open with thoughts, feelings," "gentle," "ambitious," and "assertive." And in fact, a majority of those polled (60 percent of women, 53 percent of men) said they believed that the battle of the sexes will be resolved by the turn of the century.

The justice system is also playing a key role. In 1982, Ann Hopkins, a management consultant at Price Waterhouse, was turned down for a partnership at the firm because she wasn't feminine enough. Tough, assertive, and highly talented, Hopkins had generated more new business for the company than any of the other eighty-seven partnership candidates, all of whom were men. Some of her staff accused her of being harsh, impatient, excessively demanding, and too "macho."

One partner said she needed a "course at charm school"; another (who supported her) advised her to wear make-up and jewelry, have her hair styled, and "walk more femininely, talk more femininely, and dress more femininely." Hopkins eventually sued Price Waterhouse and won her case.

Even the military is showing signs of progress. Betty Friedan, who worked with the first female graduates at West Point, reports in *The Second Stage*, "In every company and squad where women cadets actually were present, the hostility declined during the training and barracks life with the men. The reality of women's presence changed things—the hostility, the prejudice remained only in companies where women were not as present."

More recently, Army First Lieutenant Phoebe Jetter, commander of a Patriot missile battery, was the first soldier to shoot down a scud missile in what reporters called "the Moms' War." Lieutenant Betty Carr, one of thirty-five thousand women who served in the Persian Gulf, said in an interview, "There were over a thousand men and women in my group, and if a reporter made the mistake of mentioning only 'the men' serving here, there would be boos from both the women and the men." And Kay Likely, a combat supply specialist and a grandmother, told *Mirabella* magazine, "I think women really proved themselves as equals to men in this war, and that will carry for us when the war is over. The only difference between us and the men is that we hold hands whenever there's a scud attack or incoming artillery."

But the news is not all good. In *Watching America: What Television Tells Us About Our Lives*, author Robert Lichter found that women haven't made much progress in fields such as medicine and politics over the last thirty years—at least in television land. Analyzing randomly selected episodes of 620 entertainment series over a thirty-year period, Lichter found that the overall number of female characters increased by only

11 percent. In the fifties and sixties, 6 percent of television doctors were women; since 1975, the number increased only by two percentage points. In real life, however, the number of female doctors rose by 37 percent within the same time period. Another observation: women portrayed as housewives on television has decreased only slightly in thirty years (by 6 percent). In real life, as of 1988, only 27 percent of all women were homemakers.

There's also a double standard still evident in the print media. For example, *Working Woman* magazine Editor-In-Chief Katie White observed, "In a recent *Time* profile of a woman CEO, there was a quote from a former classmate who claimed that, as a girl, the woman had taught him how to French-kiss. It's interesting to note that recent profiles of businessmen in *Time* haven't delved into their pubescent experiences."

Women's paychecks are still less than men's in every field—even those dominated by women. According to statistics, women earn just 72 cents for every dollar a man earns—up just 8 cents from a decade ago.

Finally, despite the fact that female voters outnumber male voters, and that the number of women throwing their hats into the political ring has never been higher, opinion polls show that many voters are still reluctant to vote for a woman. Marie Morse, political director of the National Women's Political Caucus, said in an interview with *New Woman*, "People view men as more able to handle fiscal and military matters and women as more adept at family and social issues."

Geraldine Ferraro's campaign for the vice-presidency in 1984 is a good example. During her debate with George Bush, Ferraro was confident, articulate, and in control. She didn't hesitate to say yes when asked if she could push the nuclear button. And she stood up to Bush when he lost his temper. Yet, pollsters declared Bush the "winner." The morning after the debate, Barbara Bush called her husband's opponent "something that rhymes with rich." Ferraro was also labeled by a Reagan aide as a "nasty woman" who would "claw Ronald Reagan's eyes out."

Ann Richards's victory in the 1990 governor's race in Texas against Clayton Williams, a good ole boy and self-proclaimed male chauvinist, is another good example. Once during the campaign, Richards mentioned a poll narrowing the gap between her and her opponent, to which Williams replied, "She must be drinking again." Since Richards, a recovering alcoholic, had just celebrated her tenth year of sobriety, the voting public should have been outraged at Williams's insensitive remark. Yet, men still favored him two to one.

Sound discouraging? Perhaps. But don't take it personally. What all this boils down to is a complex web of socialization, expectation, and perception. Naturally, all of us are more likely to pay attention to people who express themselves forcefully, and men have been socially conditioned to do just that. Consequently, we *perceive* them as powerful communicators. We *expect* them to display confidence and conviction.

On the flip side, women have been taught to be polite, cooperative, and compliant. We're not *perceived* as powerful communicators. And, as a result, society sets higher *expectations* for us to meet when we try and prove ourselves otherwise. But these are expectations that women can meet—and even surpass—by becoming powerful communicators.

CHAPTER 14

The Confidence Quotient

"No one can make you feel inferior without your consent."

Eleanor Roosevelt

Learning to speak the language of power requires confidence. However, many women are perceived as being deficient in this area. For example, a survey of eight thousand men by Alma Baron, Ph.D., turned up seven reasons men gave for not wanting a female boss. Topping that list was, "She's not confident" and "She doesn't have clout—real power." But the bottom line in power communications *is* confidence, for when you believe in yourself and what you are saying, your voice, facial expression, and stance reflect that. So there's a Catch-22 at work here, but not to worry. Here are some tips to help boost your self-esteem as you learn to sharpen your power communication skills:

• Use a person's name when you are talking to them—particularly if you've just met or don't know them well. Calling a person by name is the best way to get—and keep—someone's attention. In business settings use a person's last name (preceded by Mr. or Ms.) unless they ask you to do otherwise. In social settings, using a first name is usually permissible. When in doubt, ask, "May I call you Janet?"

• Never underestimate the power of a simple handshake. According to Lester Minsuk of the outplacement firm of Minsuk, Macklin, Stein and Associates in Princeton, New Jersey, "Since women have not been socialized to shake hands, they are often unsure of when and how to do it, and their uncertainty may come across in their body language. Yet, if women want to get ahead in business, they need to learn how to shake hands confidently with fully extended fingers and a flat palm." So make it a habit to initiate a firm and professional handshake whenever you're introduced to someone or encounter someone (including another woman) you haven't seen for a while. Also use it to congratulate others as well as to confirm agreements. And if extending your hand first makes you fear being perceived as aggressive, don't worry about it. Simply give the other person an opportunity to be the one to withdraw his hand first. That way you create a balance of power.

• Use specific (versus general) language to get a point across. Specific language entails words and statements that are short, simple, direct, familiar, and concise. Instead of telling your staff, "I hope everyone will work together to get this annual report out by the end of the month," say, "The annual report is due on the thirtieth, and I need everyone's notes by the twenty-fifth." Or, instead of saying, "I think it's time I got some time off," say, "Since I put in thirty hours of overtime to finish the report this week, I'd like to have Monday off."

• Begin statements with *I, my, I want, I need*, as these connote power and decisiveness.

• Avoid verbal clutter when you speak. As speech coach Marion Woodall, author of *How To Talk So Men Will Listen*, puts it, "Poor communicators tend to talk in paragraphs. Successful communicators tend to talk in short sentences and even in bulleted items." Thus, when you are pitching an idea, keep details to a minimum. In her book, Tannen notes that women give details because doing so aids in establishing intimacy, but men generally find this trait irritating.

• Create visibility for yourself. Volunteer for a committee. Give a presentation. Develop a brochure or PR packet for your operation. Write an article for the company newsletter, your local newspaper, or a trade journal. Run for office in an organization related to your line of work. Volunteer to give a workshop in your area of expertise.

• Find a mentor who is visible and with whom you can increase your visibility by association. Good mentors will not only introduce you to key players in your organization, they will also serve as excellent sources of inside information. Furthermore, a new study of women executives shows that women with mentors get more promotions faster.

• Join a women's network. This will give you a chance to pass your business card around to other women and make important contacts. You'll also learn about job opportunities.

• Attend seminars, professional meetings, and conventions in your field. Maintain a list of any contacts you make.

• Stay in touch with colleagues you meet at meetings and conventions as well as those you've worked with in the past. Periodically, send them information you think might interest them, and call on them for ideas when you have a problem you can't solve.

• Don't be afraid to ask questions when you don't know or understand an assignment. Making inaccurate assumptions for fear of being perceived as ignorant can be far more damaging to your career than taking the time and making the effort to thoroughly understand what is expected of you.

• Read trade journals to stay on top of what's going on in your field. When you come across an article that is particularly informative, route it through the office, and ask that it be returned to you. That way, everyone knows who sent it. Or, send a copy of it to your boss with a short note saying, "Thought you'd enjoy reading this."

• Find out what makes your organization tick. Study your company's policies and procedures. Get involved in interdepartmental discussion groups or committees. Invite someone from another department or division to lunch. Make good contacts on every level of your organization.

• Make yourself indispensable. Sally, an executive secretary in the banking industry, says, "I boosted my confidence by thoroughly learning about our office equipment. When we switched computer systems, I pored over the manual and learned the tricks and shortcuts. I mastered the switchboard, even though I didn't need to. I knew the guts of our copy machine, fax machine, et cetera. Then whenever there was a problem, everyone came to me. This gave me respect. Knowledge is power."

• Create a niche for yourself by volunteering for a job nobody else wants.

• Take advantage of corporate training opportunities offered both on the job and off. And if you take a course offered by your company, be sure to write a thank-you note to your firm's president briefly summarizing what you got out of the program. Also, volunteer to train others with information you received.

• Be your own publicity agent when you've accomplished something. Send out press releases describing your achievements to your local newspapers.

• Be well-informed. Develop a conversational knowledge of world events, the stock market, the government, and sports by reading at least one daily newspaper and watching the nightly news on television.

• Look for specific problems in your area, then take specific steps (and document them) to solve them.

• Always be prepared to take the next step. Reach slightly beyond what you think are your abilities, and you will find new abilities surfacing.

• Learn how to take a compliment by saying "thank-you" instead of appearing modest or fishing for more compliments.

• Fake it until you make it. Use effective verbal and non-verbal strategies to project the image of confidence, even if you don't feel it.

• Take on challenges. If someone asks you to tackle a tough project, don't say, "I can't do that," or "I've never done that." Give it your best shot. Others believe in you because you've given them a reason to. Believe in yourself!

• Keep a weekly log of your achievements. Use it to update your résumé and to cite your accomplishments during job interviews and performance appraisals.

• When someone compliments you for a job well done, ask them to put it in writing. Then keep a file of letters you can refer to when you need references—or when your self-esteem is sorely in need of a boost.

• Be positive. If you tell yourself, "I'm a power communicator," you're more likely to be one.

CHAPTER 15

(Most Commonly Asked) Questions and Answers

More Power To You evolved from a series of communication seminars given over the past decade. In these seminars, participants were encouraged to ask specific questions. We've selected the best of these to share with you.

Q. I have a boss who is very critical. Sometimes when he's in a really bad mood, he takes everything out on me. Do you have any tips for handling criticism? I tend to hear him out then run to the bathroom for a good cry.

A. One of the reasons your boss picks on you may be because he knows he can upset you, and that makes him feel powerful. The best way to "fight back" is to use a combination of powerful verbal and nonverbal skills.

For instance, the most important thing to do when you're the object of criticism is to maintain steady eye contact. Looking away, especially down, will imply weakness and submissiveness. Frequent blinking connotes nervousness, and oftentimes, guilt.

Also try to maintain a neutral facial expression. A smile should only be used in pleasant experiences—and being the target of criticism certainly doesn't qualify! Avoid slouching or folding your arms as well, as this kind of body language makes you appear timid.

Use phrases like, "It was my understanding that . . ." or "Here are the reasons why I did it this way" to defend yourself, but remember that the tone of your voice will play a major role in the communication of emotion. In other words, if you talk too fast and in a high-pitched voice, you signal hysteria or helplessness. So concentrate on speaking evenly and in a low pitch.

Q. As an auditor, my job forces me to work alone most of the time. However, I do attend weekly meetings with my superiors. Any suggestions on how I can gain more visibility at these meetings?

A. Yes. First, sit where you can be best seen and heard. Research indicates that high-status individuals select the most focal position in a group. So try to sit at, or as close as possible to the head of the table.

Second, use powerful mannerisms and speech patterns. While listening, refrain from smiling (unless someone is saying something funny) and bobbing your head. Also avoid fiddling with jewelry or your hair, tapping a pen or pencil, or doodling on a notepad. If you have something to say, say it concisely using a moderate tone of voice and a relatively low pitch. For additional tips, review Chapter 6.

Q. I'm only twenty-five, and have been lucky to accomplish a lot in my career so far. The problem is, I'm very modest—

particularly in interview situations. How can I learn to expound on my virtues without sounding conceited?

A. The idea that women shouldn't blow their own horns—except when talking with family or close friends—can be chalked up to social conditioning. Since little boys play in large and hierarchical groups, they are expected to boast in order to establish their place in the group. Girls, however, play in small and egalitarian groups, in which bragging violates the group's ethics. Yet, as adults, men often mistake women's modesty as a genuine lack of self-confidence.

Your best bet, then, is to list and review your many accomplishments, then practice discussing them until you build up an excess of confidence and pride. And remember, if you really want a job, the best way to go after it is to explain why you're the best candidate. That's what the interviewer *expects* to hear.

Q. I work for an art gallery and must often help my boss serve as hostess for the opening receptions we have. This may sound like a silly question, but what are the proper ways to introduce people to each other?

A. There are two basic rules of etiquette concerning proper introductions that can be applied to almost any social situation. First, always mention the person of higher authority first. Also, if that person is your boss, never use her first name when introducing her to someone, unless she has requested you to do so. Second, when introducing an older person to someone younger, name the older person first.

Try to say something about people after introducing them. For example, you might mention what each one does for a living, or cite something the two people have in common.

Q. Every year I make it a point to attend as many conventions and meetings in my field as I can afford. While I enjoy the seminars and lectures, the social events make me nervous because I can't ever seem to remember people's names. Any tips?

A. This happens to the best of us and usually occurs because we didn't hear a person's name in the first place. Experts who have studied the memory process advise that whenever you are introduced to someone, concentrate on the person's name, repeat it aloud (as in, "It's nice to meet you, *Carol*"), then make a visual association that will help you remember it. For example, maybe Carol has a sweet and soft voice that reminds you of a Christmas carol. So try these tips next time you meet someone.

In the meantime, if you've forgotten someone's name whom you've met before, be calm and straightforward. But *don't* say, "I've forgotten your name." Instead, say something like, "I remember meeting you, but I simply can't recall your name."

And if you sense someone else has forgotten *your* name, rescue them by saying, "Hi, I'm Barbara. We met at. . . ."

Q. After five years of working as a secretary, I was recently promoted to office manager. I was very excited about my position—until my boss demanded that I reprimand a former colleague for being late three weeks in a row turning in weekly sales figures. Looking back, I think I botched it. Are there positive ways to reprimand someone?

A. Yes. For starters, you want to communicate a sense of calmness and professionalism through your body language and speech patterns. So don't wring your hands, hang your head, smile, or act as if you're about to drop a bomb. Establish and maintain good eye contact, face the employee, and lean slightly toward her.

Keep your voice low and even; don't sound accusatory or

use sarcasm. Remember to criticize *behaviors*, not people, and stick to the specific issue at hand. Avoid using phrases like, "You *always* turn your figures in late," or "You *never* turn your materials in on time." Instead, use phrases like, "*It is my impression that* you've been late turning in your figures these last few weeks because you've been devoting most of your time to the Haynes account," or "*Let's talk this over so we can* find ways to help you get your figures to me on time." And use the pronoun *I* instead of *you*. Don't say, "*You* are not turning in your figures on time," but "*I* can't get my report out on time unless *I* get your figures."

Q. I have recently been appointed to sit on the finance committee at work. As an estate planner, I have a lot of expertise in this area and a lot of good ideas. The problem is, I'm the only woman on the committee, and whenever I speak up, I get interrupted. What can I do to solve this problem, short of acting rude like these men?

A. There's nothing quite so unnerving or frustrating as being interrupted when you're trying to make a point. And studies show that men interrupt us more than we interrupt them. In fact, one study that compared conversations between men and women with those between just men showed that interruptions in all-male conversations were balanced between the speakers. However, in the male-female pairs, the men interrupted women 96 percent more than women interrupted men!

Yet, men are not totally to blame for this phenomenon. Thanks to social conditioning, women tend to allow interruptions. We are also reluctant to speak up when we're cut off in the middle of a conversation, because doing so would require interruption on our part—and that would be impolite. As a result, men often assume we have nothing of importance to say.

The trick to keeping interruptions to a minimum is to use assertive body language and speech patterns. For example, according to an article in *Discover* magazine, a study of former British Prime Minister Margaret Thatcher showed that she was interrupted more frequently—even by men who ranked below her—whenever she dropped her eyes, looked away, or dropped her volume and paused. So when you're interrupted, maintain eye contact with the person or people you're talking to, and raise the volume of your voice slightly. Avoid looking at the interrupter, and if he continues talking, hold your hand up in a "stop sign" gesture to signal that you're not finished talking.

If these strategies don't work, look briefly at the interrupter and say, "I'm not finished," or "Just a minute, please." Do *not* apologize or say, "Please excuse me, but . . ." In fact, the fewer qualifiers you use, the less you'll be interrupted.

Q. I've recently taken my first job as a secretary in a small advertising firm. Do I need a business card?

A. You do if you aspire to moving up in—and even out of— your field. Business cards are an inexpensive way to let people know who you are and what you do. And since you work for an advertising firm, consider making your business card stand out by using a touch of creativity to show others who you are.

Q. Last year, I got a big promotion. My boss says I'm doing well, but I'm not so sure. This is a whole new area for me, and I'm at a level I never dreamed I'd reach. Everyone says I've caught on fast, but I get so frustrated whenever I make a mistake. In fact, many times I feel convinced that one morning I'm going to walk in and find a replacement sitting at my desk. My friends keep telling me I'm the victim of the "imposter syndrome." What does this mean, and how can I overcome it?

A. "Imposter syndrome" relates to successful women's tendencies to believe that they've gotten where they are due to luck or chance rather than as the result of hard work. It's a very common phenomenon among women. In fact, according to Pauline Rose Clance, Ph.D., author of *The Imposter Phenomenon: Overcoming the Fear That Haunts Your Success*, some 70 percent of successful people in this country feel that their success is undeserved. "In spite of promotions and praise, they attribute their success to good timing, connections, being in the 'right place at the right time,' and just plain luck," she says. "They live with the constant fear that at some point they'll be discovered and their lack of real competence will be revealed."

Not surprisingly, victims of this malady are more often women than men. Lee Bell and Valerie Young, who give career-related workshops on this topic, say, "Imposters, Fakes, and Frauds" was developed in response to the "surprisingly vast number of bright and capable women who, despite external evidence to the contrary, continue to doubt their confidence. By downplaying or dismissing their abilities and accomplishments, such women are often stymied in their careers. They operate with the disabling belief that they are, in effect, imposters, or fakes, or frauds."

There are several steps you can take to break the imposter cycle. First, ease up on yourself. Don't expect perfection. Instead, recognize that everyone makes mistakes and try to view them as learning opportunities rather than failures. Second, listen closely to the praise and compliments others give you. Write these down after they occur, and refer back to your list in moments of doubt. Finally, consider taking a workshop on bolstering your self-esteem or dealing with success. Many local colleges and universities now offer such courses through their continuing education departments. All of these strategies should help you to focus on the fact that you landed a big promotion because you *deserved* it!

Q. I live and work in a small town, where professional positions for women are rare. Still, I hope to start my own business someday and think I could learn a lot from networking with other women. What can I do if there are no women's networking groups where I live?

A. You might have to travel to a nearby town or rely on making contacts with other professional women by attending meetings and conferences in your field. Or, you could start a smaller network of your own by organizing quarterly get-togethers for all the businesswomen in your area.

Q. I'm one of two "token" women in the city government office of a medium-sized town. It seems whenever we have staff meetings, and one of us comes up with an idea, we are ignored. It's as if we're invisible! Why does this happen?

A. More than likely, it's *how* you're pitching your ideas that's the problem. For example, Deborah Tannen, Ph.D., author of the best-seller *You Just Don't Understand: Women and Men in Conversation*, acknowledges that often a woman at a meeting will make a comment that is ignored, only to have a male colleague make the same point and have it taken seriously. Tannen says that part of the reason for this may be "that the woman presented her point in a stereotypically feminine way—she spoke briefly, phrased it as a question, spoke at a low volume and a high pitch. If the man who followed her used a stereotypically masculine style of speaking—he spoke at length, in a loud, declamatory voice—his message was the same, but the metamessage was different: 'This is important.' ''

Q. I have been stuck in a dead-end job for four years. Now I've been offered a chance to take a lateral move into an area I'm not trained in, but it is one I'm interested in and think would be a better steppingstone. Should I take the risk?

A. By all means! A landmark three-year study of female executives, conducted by the Center for Creative Leadership, found that male executives take notice of women who change jobs or take on new assignments—particularly when new roles broaden their perspective and job knowledge. In addition, senior executives put a high premium on women who take risks. "Perhaps risk taking means more to executives when exhibited by a woman than a man, since women, according to stereotype, aren't expected to take risks," the study's authors state.

Q. Since being promoted from sales representative to sales manager six months ago, I've had trouble dealing with one of my subordinates. She, too, had applied for the position and was angry when I was chosen over her. Now she refuses to cooperate with me. I've tried talking to her about the problem, but she has such a poor attitude that I lose my temper every time we sit down to talk. How can I keep my cool?

A. First, try to talk to her in neutral territory. For example, consider taking her out to lunch. Next, be empathic. Tell her you understand how she must feel, but *don't* apologize for winning the job over her. *Do* tell her that you value her contributions to the company, and that you are looking for ways to work out the problems you two are experiencing.

Third, ask her for suggestions on how to solve the problems and when she starts to talk, use powerful listening skills.

Q. Since I've been a "professional" person a lot longer than I've been a "family" person, I still have a hard time communicating my personal versus professional needs on the job. How do you communicate with your colleagues about conflicts between the two? How much do you leave unsaid? Is it okay to cancel meetings when your family need is high? Do you give the reasons for canceling (for example, a sick child)?

A. This is a tough issue for women and the answer for you depends on your colleagues' and boss's perspective. If, for example, they are parents too, they are more likely to show understanding when a conflict arises—provided you don't make a habit of it and provided you still meet your commitments.

In an article for *Working Mother* magazine, Susan Mercandetti, a producer for ABC's *Nightline*, explores this issue and offers this advice. "Know your worth to the company." In other words, if you're a valuable player, your superiors will be far more tolerant of your taking time off for personal reasons. "It is legitimate for working moms to ask for more flexibility," Mercandetti adds. "But women must lay the groundwork beforehand. They have to put in time at a job and prove themselves."

As for where to draw the line between your personal and professional life when communicating with colleagues, be careful here. Motherhood is a rewarding experience, but at work your conversations should focus more on professional topics than personal ones. Certainly, you can make passing remarks about your children, but don't overdo it. Otherwise, you risk not being perceived as career oriented.

References/
Bibliography

Introduction

Survey conducted by Communispond, Inc. Reported in *Training/Human Resouces Development*. October 1981.

Chapter 1: In the Beginning

Bell, L. and V. Young. Imposters, Fakes, and Frauds. In: L.L. Moore (ed.) *Not As Far As You Think: The Realities of Working Women*. Lexington Books, Lexington MA. 1976.

Bender, D.L. and B. Leone. *Male/Female Roles*. Greenhaven Press, St. Paul, MN. 1989.

Busby, L.J. 1974. Defining the Sex-role Standards in Network Children's Programs. *Journalism Quarterly* 51:690–696.

Crandall, V.J. Sex Differences in Expectancy of Intellectual and Academic Reinforcement. In: C.P. Smith (ed.) *Achievement-related Motives in Children*. New York: Russell Sage. 1969.

Freize, I.H. Women's Expectations for and Causal Attributions of Success and Failure. In: M. Mednick, S. Tangri, and L. Hoffman (eds.) *Women and Achievement*. New York: Wiley. 1975.

Kramarae, C. *Women and Men Speaking*. Rowley, MA: Newbury House. 1981.

Lever, J. 1976. Sex Differences in the Games Children Play. *Social Problems* 23:478–483.

Lips, H.M. and N.L. Colwill. *The Psychology of Sex Differences*. Englewood Cliffs, NJ: Prentice-Hall. 1978.

Moore, L.L. *Not As Far As You Think: The Realities of Working Women*. Lexington Books, Lexington, MA. 1976.

Nichols, J.C. 1975. Causal Attributions and Other Achievement-related Cognitions: Effects of Task Outcome, Attainment, Value and Sex. *Journal of Personality and Social Psychology* 31:379–389.

Nilson, A. 1971. Women in Children's Literature. *College English* 33:918–926.

Paley, V. *Boys and Girls: Superheroes in the Doll Corner*. Chicago: University of Chicago Press. 1984.

Rubin, J.Z., F.J. Provenzano, and Z. Luria. 1974. The Eye of the Beholder: Parents' Views on Sex of Newborns. *American Journal of Orthopsychiatry* 44(4):512–519.

Serbin, L.A., D.K. O'Leary, R.N. Kent, and I. Tonck. 1973. A Comparison of Teacher Response to the Problem and Preacademic Behavior of Boys and Girls. *Child Development* 44:796–804.

Tanenbaum, J. *Male and Female Realities: Understanding the Opposite Sex*. Candle Publishing Co., Sugarland, TX 1989.

Weitzman, L. 1972. Sex-role Socialization in Picture Books for Preschool Children. *American Journal of Sociology* 77:1125–50.

Will, J., P. Self, and N. Datan. 1976. Maternal Behavior and Perceived Sex of Infant. *American Journal of Orthopsychiatry* 46:135–139.

Chapter 2: Speech Patterns
That Give You Away

Ailes, R. *You Are the Message: Getting What You Want By Being Who You Are*. New York: Doubleday. 1988.

Brownmiller, S. *Femininity*. Linden Press/Simon & Schuster. New York, NY 1984.

Carr-Ruffino, N. *The Promotable Woman: Becoming A Successful Manager*. Belmont, CA: Wadsworth. 1985.

DeVito, J.A. and M.L. Hecht. *The Nonverbal Communication Reader*. Waveland Press. Prospect Heights, IL 1990.

Eakins, B.W. and R.G. Eakins. *Sex Differences in Human Communication*. Boston: Houghton Mifflin. 1987.

Fishman, P. Interaction: The Work Women Do. *Social Problems* 25:397–406.

Frick, R.W. 1985. Communication Emotion: The Role of Prosodic Features. *Psychological Bulletin* 97:412–429.

Hirschman, L. Female-Male Differences in Conversational Interaction. Abstracted in: B. Thorne and N. Henley's *Language and Sex: Difference and Dominance*. Rowley, MA: Newbury House. 1975.

Hunsaker, J. and P. Hunsaker. *Strategies and Skills for Managerial Women*. South-Western Publishing Co. Cincinnati, OH 1986.

Lakoff, R. *Language and Woman's Place*. New York: Harper & Row. 1975.

Linver. S. *Speakeasy: How to Talk Your Way to the Top*. New York: Summit Books. 1978.

Nelson-Schneider, A. Interview. August 1991.

Tannen, D. *You Just Don't Understand: Women and Men in Conversation*. New York: Morrow. 1990.

Woodall, M.K. *How To Talk So Men Will Listen*. New York: Warner Books. 1992.

Chapter 3: Mannerisms to Make You a Heavyweight

Amalfitano, J.G. and N.C. Kalt. 1977. Effects of Eye Contact on the Evaluation of Job Applicants. *Journal of Employment Counseling* 14:46–48.

Bitler, S. *Professional Image*. New York: Putnam. 1984.

Carr-Ruffino, N. *The Promotable Woman: Becoming A Successful Manager*. Belmont, CA: Wadsworth. Prospect Heights, IL 1985.

Eakins, B.W. and R. G. Eakins. *Sex Differences in Human Communication*. Boston: Houghton Mifflin. 1978.

Elsea, J.G. *The Four-Minute Sell*. New York: Simon & Schuster. 1984.

Dellinger, S. and B. Deane. *Communicating Effectively: A Complete Guide for Better Managing*. Chilton Book Co. Radnor, PA. 1982.

DeVito, J.A. and M.L. Hecht. *The Nonverbal Communication Reader*. Waveland Press. 1990.

Kennedy, C.W. and C. Camden. 1983. Interruptions and Nonverbal Gender Differences. *Journal of Nonverbal Behavior* 8: 91–108.

Key, M.R. *Male/Female Language*. Metuchen, NJ: The Scarecrow Press, Inc. 1975.

Mehrabian, A. *Nonverbal Communication*. Chicago: Aldine-Atherton. 1972.

Molloy, J.T. *Live for Success*. New York: Warner Books. 1981.

McGovern, T.V. 1986. The Making of a Job Interviewee: The Effect of Nonverbal Behavior on an Interviewer's Evaluations During a Selection Interview. *Dissertation Abstracts International*, 4740B.

Park, M.B. 1979. Women Smile Less for Success. *Psychology Today*. March 1979, p. 16.

Shannon, J. 1987. Don't Smile When You Say That. *Executive Female* 10:33–43.

Chapter 4: Male Talk

Harragan, B.L. *Games Mother Never Taught You: Corporate Gamesmanship for Women*. New York: Rawson Associates. 1977.

Schellhardt, T.D. For Managing Insight, Try Box Scores at Breakfast. *The Wall Street Journal*. April 29, 1991.

Urbanska, W. Women in Politics. *New Woman*. November 1990, pp. 108–112.

Reinhardt, C. Lessons from the Poker Table. *Working Woman*. February 1991, p. 52.

Chapter 5: Podium Power

Austin, N.K. The Subtle Signals of Success. *Working Woman*. April 1991, pp. 80–106.

Austin, N.K. Why Listening Isn't as Easy as It Sounds. *Working Woman*. March 1991, p. 46.

Detz, J. *How to Write and Give a Speech*. New York: St. Martin's. 1984.

Hoff, R. *I Can See You Naked: A Fearless Guide to Making Great Presentations*. Andrews & McMeel/Universal Press. Kansas City, MO. 1988.

Kleck, R.E. and W. Nuessle. 1968. Congruence Between the Indicative and Communicative Functions of Eye Contact in Interpersonal Relationships. *British Journal of Social and Clinical Psychology* 7:241–246.

Kushner, M.L. *The Light Touch: How to Use Humor for Business Success*. New York: Simon & Schuster. 1990.

Landers, A. *Athens Daily News*. May 1, 1991.

Lynch, R. Interview. December, 1991.

Peoples, D.A. *Presentations Plus*. New York: Wiley. 1988.

Parkhurst, W. *The Eloquent Executive: A Guide to High Impact Speaking in Big Meetings, Small Meetings, and One-on-One*. New York: Times Books. 1988.

Rafe, S.C. *How to Be Prepared to Think on Your Feet*. Harper Business 1990.

Spivak, H. The Art of Standing Out in a Crowd. *Working Woman*. June 1991, pp. 66–69.

Tannen, D. *You Just Don't Understand: Women and Men in Conversation*. New York: Morrow. 1990.

Wallechinsky, D., I. Wallace, and A. Wallace. *The Book of Lists*. New York: Morrow. 1977.

What Enhances Your Career. *Communication Briefings*. January 1991, p. 1 (survey of subscribers).

Chapter 6: Mastering Meetings

Bitler, S. *Professional Image*. New York: Putnam. 1984.

Cole, D. Meetings That Make Sense. *Psychology Today*. May 1989, pp. 14–15.

Dellinger, S. and B. Deane. *Communicating Effectively: A Complete Guide for Better Managing*. Chilton Book Co. Radnor, PA. 1982.

DeVito, J.A. and M.L. Hecht. *The Nonverbal Communication Reader*. Waveland Press. Prospect Heights, IL. 1990.

Kieffer, G.D. *The Strategy of Meetings*. New York: Simon & Schuster. 1988.

Lott, D.F. and R. Sommer. 1967. Seating Arrangements and Status. *Journal of Personality and Social Psychology* 7:90–95.

Meyer, H.D. *Lifetime Encyclopedia of Letters*. Englewood Cliffs, NJ: Prentice-Hall. 1983.

Parkhurst, W. *The Eloquent Executive: A Guide to High Impact Speaking in Big Meetings, Small Meetings, and One-on-One*. New York: Times Books. 1988.

Sarnoff, D. *Making the Most of Your Best: A Complete Program for Presenting Yourself and Your Ideas with Confidence and Authority*. New York: Holt, Rinehart & Winston. 1981.

Schabacker, K.A Short, Snappy Guide to Meaningful Meetings. *Working Woman*. June 1991, pp. 70–73.

Strodtbeck. F.L. and L.H. Hook. 1961. The Social Dimensions of a Twelve-man Jury Table. *Sociometry* 24:297–315.

Thomsett, M.C. *The Little Black Book of Business Meetings*. New York: AMACOM. 1989.

Trahey, J. *Women and Power*. New York: Avon Books. 1977.

Chapter 7: The Write Track

Cooper, G. (ed.) *Red Tape Holds Up New Bridge and More Flubs from the Nation's Press*. New York: Peregrine Books. 1987.

Englander, T. 1988. Management Reports That Make You Look Good. *Meetings and Conventions.* August 1988, pp. 91–94.

Leno, J. (ed.) *More Headlines.* New York: Warner Books. 1990.

Maccoby, E.E. and C.N. Jacklin. *The Psychology of Sex Differences.* Stanford University Press. Stanford, CA. 1974.

Macrorie, K. *Telling Writing.* Third Edition. Rochelle Park, NJ: Hayden Book Co. 1980.

McCormack, M.H. *What They Don't Teach You at Harvard Business School.* Toronto; New York: Bantam Books. 1984.

McCormack, M.H. *What They Still Don't Teach You at Harvard Business School.* Toronto; New York: Bantam Books. 1989.

McKellar, P. *Imagination and Thinking.* New York: Basic Books. 1957.

Parkhurst, W. *The Eloquent Executive: A Guide to High Impact Speaking in Big Meetings, Small Meetings, and One-on-One.* New York: Times Books. 1988.

Shepherd, C., J.J. Kohut, and R. Sweet. *News of the Weird.* New York: Penguin Books. 1989.

Strunk, W. and E.B. White. *The Elements of Style.* Third Edition. Macmillan. 1979.

Westheimer, P.H. *Power Writing for Executive Women.* Glenview, IL: Scott, Foresman. 1989.

What Enhances Your Career. *Communication Briefings.* January 1991, p. 1 (survey of subscribers).

Chapter 8: Lighten Up!
The Power of Humor

Barreca, R. *They Used to Call Me Snow White . . . But I Drifted: Women's Strategic Use of Humor*. New York: Viking. 1991.

Cohen, S.S. *Tender Power*. Reading MA: Addison-Wesley. 1989.

Copetas, C. and S.C. Hargrove. Conquering Heroines. *Mirabella*. June 1991, pp. 26–35.

Coser, R.L. 1960. Laughter Among Colleagues. *Psychiatry* 13:81–95.

Deutsch, C., Communications Consultant, Asheville, North Carolina. (Interview).

Friedan, B. *The Second Stage*. New York: Summit Books. 1981.

Goodman, J. Interview. August 1991.

Suskind, R.A Lady Lawyer in Laramie Writes a Landmark Letter; Becky Klemt's Put-down of High-priced Colleagues Brings Her Global Fame. *The Wall Street Journal*. September 6, 1990.

Kushner, M.L. *The Light Touch: How to Use Humor for Business Success*. New York: Simon & Schuster. 1990.

Landers, A. *The Athens Daily News*. August 9, 1990.

Mackoff, B. *What Mona Lisa Knew: A Woman's Guide to Getting Ahead in Business by Lightening Up*. Los Angeles: Lowell House. 1990.

McGhee, P.E. The Role of Laughter and Humor in Growing Up Female. In: C.B. Kopp (ed.) *Becoming Female: Perspectives on Development*. New York: Plenum Press. 1979.

Porterfield, K.M. Funny Business. *Braniff Destinations*. September 1985, pp. 9–10.

Richman, A. Gerald Ford's Humor Symposium Recalls a

Stumbling Presidency, But Proves He's a Stand-up Guy. *People*. October 6, 1986.

Russell, A.M. and L. Calvacca. Should You Be Funny at Work? *Working Woman*. March 1991, pp. 74–128.

Tanenbaum, J. *Male and Female Realities: Understanding the Opposite Sex*. Candle Publishing Co. Sugarland, TX. 1989.

Tannen, D. *You Just Don't Understand: Women and Men in Conversation*. New York: Morrow. 1990.

The Real Murphy Brown Hears Her Clock Tick. *People*. Extra Edition. *Inside Hollywood: Women, Sex and Power*. Spring 1991, pp. 63–64.

Twidale, H. 1986. Nowadays Being "Old Sourpuss" Is No Joke. *Working Woman*. March 1986, p. 18.

Wade, C. Humor. In: C. Tavris (ed.) *Everywoman's Emotional Well-being*. New York: Doubleday. 1986.

Chapter 9: Strategic Listening

Austin, N.K. Why Listening's Not as Easy as It Sounds. *Working Woman*. March 1991, pp. 46–48.

Bone, D. *The Business of Listening: A Practical Guide to Effective Listening*. Los Altos, CA: Crisp Pubications. 1988.

Cole, D. Say What? Paying Attention Can Pay Off. *Chicago Sun-Times*. June 12, 1991.

Elsea, J.G. *The Four-Minute Sell*. New York: Simon & Schuster. 1984.

Fallon, W.K. *Effective Communication on the Job*. Los Altos, CA: Crisp Publications. 1988.

Hoffman, G. and P. Graivier. *Speak the Language of Success: A Handbook for Communications Skills*. New York: Putnam. 1983.

McGhee, P.E. The Role of Laughter and Humor in Growing Up Female. In: C.B. Kopp (ed.) *Becoming Female: Perspectives on Development*. New York: Plenum Press. 1979.

Chapter 10: First Impressions

Bixler, S. *The Professional Image*. New York: Putnam. 1984.

Buffington, P.W. Lasting Impressions. *Sky*. October 1987, pp. 65–70.

Carle, G. Interview. August 1991.

Efran, M.G. 1974. The Effect of Physical Appearance on the Judgement of Guilt, Interpersonal Attraction and Severity of Recommended Punishment in a Simulated Jury Task. *Journal of Experimental Research in Personality* 8:45–54.

Ekman, P. and W. Friesen. Personal Appearance Factors Which Influence Perceptions of Credibility and Approachability of Men and Women. In: L.J. Smith and L.A. Malandro (eds.) *Courtroom Strategies*. New York: Kluwer Book Publishers. 1985.

Ekman, P. and W. Friesen. *Unmasking the Face: A Guide to Recognizing Emotions from Facial Expressions*. Englewood Cliffs, NJ: Prentice-Hall. 1975.

Gorden, W.I., C.D. Tengler, and D.A. Infante. 1982. Women's Clothing Predispositions as Predictors of Dress at Work, Job Satisfaction, and Career Advancement. *Southern Speech Communication Journal* 47:422–434.

Harragan, B.L. *Games Mother Never Taught You: Corporate Gamesmanship for Women*. New York: Rawson Associates. 1977.

Korda, M. Status Marks—A Gold-plated Thermos Is Man's Best Friend. In: A.M. Katz and V.T. Katz (eds.) *Foundations of Nonverbal Communication*. Carbondale, IL: Southern Illinois University Press. 1983.

Power Dressing Is Just Icing on the Cake. Gannett Westchester Newspapers. July 11, 1990.

Roesch, R. *Smart Talk: The Art of Savvy Business Conversation*. New York: AMACOM. 1989.

Rosencrantz, M.L. *Clothing Concepts*. New York: Macmillan. 1969.

Tetlock, P.E. 1983. Accountability and the Perserverance of First Impressions. *Social Psychology Quarterly* 46: 285–292.

Chapter 11: Telephone Power

Bowers, J.T. Your Company's Image Is on the (Phone) Line. *The Wall Street Journal*. December 12, 1988.

Elsea, J.G. *The Four-Minute Sell*. New York: Simon & Schuster. 1984.

Friedman, N. Interview. August 1991.

Garner, P.A. *The Office Telephone: A User's Guide*. Englewood Cliffs, NJ: Prentice-Hall. 1984.

Goodman, G.S. *You Can Sell Anything By Telephone!* Englewood Cliffs, NJ: Prentice-Hall. 1984.

Klein, J.H. *The Phone Book: The ABC's of Successful Telephone Communications*. The Donning Company. Norfolk, VA. 1987.

Phillips, L. and W. Phillips. *The Concise Guide to Executive Etiquette*. New York: Doubleday. 1990.

Scott. D. *Time Management and the Telephone: Making It a Tool and Not a Tyrant*. Los Altos, CA: Crisp Publications. 1988.

Walther, G.R. *Phone Power: How to Make the Telephone Your Most Profitable Business Tool*. New York: Putnam. 1986.

Chapter 12: Management Style

Carle G. Interview. August 1991.

Kanter, R.M. *Men and Women of the Corporation*. New York: Basic Books. 1977.

Kanter, R.M. Women and the Structure of Organizations: Explorations in Theory and Behavior. In: M. Millman and R.M. Kanter (eds.) *Another Voice*. New York: Anchor Price. 1975.

Lenz, E. and B. Myerhoff. *The Feminization of America: How Women's Values Are Changing Our Public and Private Lives*. Los Angeles: Jeremy P. Tarcher. 1985.

Lusardi, L.A. Power Talk. Interview with Deborah Tannen. *Working Woman*. July 1990, p. 92.

McCormack, M.A. *What They Don't Teach You at Harvard Business School*. Toronto; New York: Bantam Books. 1984.

Morrison, A.M., R.P. White, E. Van Velsor, and the Center for Creative Leadership. *Breaking the Glass Ceiling*. Reading, MA: Addison-Wesley. 1987.

Naisbitt, J. and P. Aburdene. *Megatrends 2000: Ten New Directions for the 1990s*. New York: Morrow. 1990.

Nelton, S. Men and Women in Leadership. *Nation's Business*. May 1991, pp. 16–22.

Peters, T. and R.H. Waterman. *In Search of Excellence: Lessons from America's Best-run Companies*. New York: Harper & Row. 1982.

Rosener, J.B. Ways Women Lead. *Harvard Business Review*. November-December 1990, pp. 119–125.

Tannen, D. *You Just Don't Understand: Women and Men in Conversation*. New York: Morrow. 1990.

Chapter 13: The Politics of Communication

Barreca, R. *They Used to Call Me Snow White . . . But I Drifted: Women's Strategic Use of Humor*. New York: Viking. 1991.

Copetas, C. and S.C. Hargrave. Conquering Heroines. *Mirabella*. June 1991, pp. 26–35.

Desjardins, C. and C.O. Brown. A New Look at Leadership Styles. *National Forum* (Phi Kappa Phi Journal). Winter 1991, pp. 18–20.

Edwards, O. On Being a New Man. *New Woman*. October 1990, pp. 168–169.

Friedan, B. *The Second Stage*. New York: Summit Books. 1981.

Goodman, E. Meet the New Model Man: Tough and Tender. *Los Angeles Times*. March 10, 1991.

Hoffman, L.W. 1974. Maternal Employment and the Young Child. In: M. Perlmutter (ed.) *The Minnesota Symposium on Child Psychology*. Hillsdale, NJ: Lawrence Erlbaum Associates. 1984.

Lenz, E. and B. Myerhoff. *The Feminization of America: How Women's Values Are Changing Our Public and Private Lives*. Los Angeles: Jeremy P. Tarcher. 1985.

Lichter, R. *Watching America: What Television Tells Us About Our Lives*. Englewood Cliffs, NJ: Prentice-Hall. 1991.

Loden, M. *Feminine Leadership or How to Succeed in Business Without Being One of the Boys*. New York: Times Books. 1985.

Nelton, S. Men and Women in Leadership. *Nation's Business*. May 1991, pp. 16–22.

Price Waterhouse Ordered to Make Woman a Partner. *The Wall Street Journal*. May 16, 1990.

O'Conner, K. Clout Is Shifting as the Gender Gap Widens

into a Gulf. *The Atlanta Journal/The Atlanta Constitution*. May 26, 1991.

Rosener, J.B. Ways Women Lead. *Harvard Business Review*. November-December 1990, pp. 119–125.

Rubenstein, C. and S. von Hirschberg. A Brave New World. *New Woman*. October 1990, pp. 158–164.

Saltzman, A. Trouble at the Top. *U.S. News & World Report*. June 17, 1991, pp. 40–48.

Sex Still Matters. *Newsweek*. October 29, 1990, pp. 34–35.

Spock, B. *Baby and Child Care*. Revised Edition. New York: Pocket Books. 1976.

Urbanska, W. Women in Politics. *New Woman*. November 1990, pp. 108–112.

White, K. Letter From the Editor. *Working Woman*. November 1990, p. 20.

Chapter 14: The Confidence Quotient

Beatty, G.J. and D.C. Gardner. Are You a Hot Prospect? *Working Woman*. April 1991, pp. 76–79.

Cassidy, R. How We're Viewed by the Men We Boss. *Savvy*. July 1982, pp. 15–18.

Davidson, J.P. *Blow Your Own Horn: How to Market Yourself and Your Career*. New York: American Management Association. 1987.

Kanter, R.M. *Men and Women of the Corporation*. New York: Basic Books. 1977.

Mentors Help Women Succeed, Study Indicates. *The Atlanta Journal/The Atlanta Constitution*. July 21, 1991.

Shaking It on the Job. *The Atlanta Journal/The Atlanta Constitution*. August 6, 1991.

Tannen, D. *You Just Don't Understand: Women and Men in Conversation*. New York: Morrow. 1990.

Woodall, M.K. *How To Talk So Men Will Listen*. New York: Warner Books. 1992.

Chapter 15: (Most Commonly Asked) Questions & Answers

Beattie, G. et al. Invited Interruptions. *Discover*. March 1983, pp. 15–18.

Bell, L. and V. Young. Imposters, Fakes, and Frauds. In: L.L. Moore (ed.) *Not as Far as You Think: The Realities of Working Women*. Lexington Books. Lexington, MA 1986.

Brownmiller, S. *Femininity*. Linden Press/Simon & Schuster. New York, NY. 1984.

Clance, P.R. *The Imposter Phenomenon: Overcoming the Fear That Haunts Your Success*. Atlanta, GA: Peachtree Publishers. 1985.

Elsea, J.G. *The Four-Minute Sell*. New York: Simon & Schuster. 1984.

Goodwin, M.H. *He-Said-She-Said: Talk as Social Organization Among Black Children*. Bloomington, IN: Indiana University Press. 1990.

Kennedy, C.W. and C. Camden. 1983. Interruptions and Nonverbal Gender Differences. *Journal of Nonverbal Behavior* 8: 91–108.

Lenz, E. and B. Myerhoff. *The Feminization of America: How Women's Values Are Changing Our Public and Private Lives*. Los Angeles: Jeremy P. Tarcher. 1985.

Lusardi, L.A. Power Talk. Interview with Deborah Tannen. *Working Woman*. July 1990, pp. 92–94.

Mercandetti, S. T.V. Newswomen and the Mommy Flak. *Working Mother*. August 1991, pp. 8–11.

Morrison, A.M., R.P. White, E. Van Velsor, and the Center

for Creative Leadership. *Breaking the Glass Ceiling*. Reading, MA: Addison-Wesley. 1987.

Phillips, L. and W. Phillips. *The Concise Guide to Executive Etiquette*. New York: Doubleday. 1990.

Roesch, R. *Smart Talk: The Art of Savvy Business Conversation*. AMACOM 1989.

Silverstein, A. and V. Silverstein. *Wonders of Speech*. New York: Morrow. 1988.

Tannen, D. *You Just Don't Understand: Women and Men in Conversation*. New York: Morrow. 1990.

Zimmerman, D.H. and C. West. Sex Roles, Interruptions and Silences in Conversation. In: B. Thorne, and N. Henley (eds.) *Language and Sex: Difference and Dominance*. Rowley, MA: Newbury House. 1975.

About the Authors

CONNIE BROWN GLASER is a nationally recognized communications consultant and specialist in women and communications. She is a frequent guest on TV and radio talk shows, including the *Joan Rivers Show, Good Day New York*, and *Working Woman*.

Glaser's dynamic seminars have helped thousands of women to empower themselves in "breaking the glass ceiling." Her clients include Xerox Corporation, the National League of Cities, the Showtime Channel, and the Environmental Protection Agency. With a master's degree from the University of Michigan, Glaser is in special demand by business and professional women's groups around the country.

BARBARA STEINBERG SMALLY is a freelance writer based in Athens, Georgia, with over fourteen years of experience. She specializes in women's issues and is the author of more than 200 articles. Her byline has appeared in many national and international newspapers and magazines, including *Reader's Digest, New Woman, Redbook, Cosmopolitan, McCall's, Family Circle, Essence, Elle, American Way, USAir*, and *Kiwanis*. Smalley, along with Glaser, has also coauthored a weekly "On the Job" column for *Woman's World*. Smalley is a member of the National Association of Female Executives and Business and Professional Women. Recently, she was named an Outstanding Young Woman of America.

Communicate Your Way to Success!
MORE POWER TO YOU!
KEYNOTE SPEECHES • SEMINARS • WORKSHOPS

Success in any organization depends on your ability to communicate effectively with others. How you look, talk, and move affects the messages you send. Moreover, your communication skills are almost always the determining factors when you are in the running for a new position, in line for a promotion, or being considered for a pay raise. Don't let yours hold you back!

More Power To You! is an upbeat and enlightening presentation designed to help women enhance their image and credibility through effective communication skills. Here's how audiences who have participated in *More Power To You!* describe the presentation and its presenter, Connie Brown Glaser . . .

"An outstanding presentation. My only regret is that the time went by so quickly. We could have listened for at least another hour."
—Lucille Luongo, president,
American Women in Radio and Television, NY

"Connie Glaser is a dynamic, exciting, and motivating speaker. She is that rare being—a good teacher."
—John South, president, South College

"Many thanks for an excellent presentation. It was an informative, enlightening, and entertaining program."
—Rosemary Harper, vice president,
American Chamber of Commerce Executives

"Our Congress of Cities was an outstanding success, and your presentation was one of the reasons why. Thanks for your knowledge, information, and enthusiasm."
—Alan Beals, executive director, National League of Cities

For more information on *More Power To You!*
presentations, call (404) 804-0318 or (706) 613-7237.